Mastering Blazor UI

Advanced Custom Components and Design Strategies

By

David Gallivan

Table of Contents

About the Author

This book empowers you to fully leverage Blazor, enabling you to create the next generation of fully functional and professional web-based applications.

Authored by David Gallivan—a distinguished graduate of Chapman University with a degree in Computer Science and Electronics, a Microsoft Certified Solution Developer in .NET, and a seasoned software engineer with over 20 years of experience in building commercial software, from off-the-shelf products to enterprise solutions valued in the millions. David has crafted a wide range of solutions, from simple Windows desktop applications to complex, enterprise-level web-based systems. His work spans customer-facing applications, internal business tools, and more, including contributions to four software companies that he helped grow and successfully sell. Among his diverse projects, some of his favorites include the "13th Pair Free" initiative, ad-based revenue generation, and websites for musical bands. David is also the inventor behind two patented technologies, reflecting his creativity and innovation. Beyond his technical achievements, David is passionate about educating the next generation of software engineers.

In this book, David distills his extensive experience into actionable insights, offering an unparalleled guide to the art and science of developing exceptional Blazor applications.

Introduction

Blazor has emerged as a powerful framework in the world of modern web development, offering developers the ability to create interactive web applications using C# instead of JavaScript. Since its introduction, Blazor has rapidly evolved, becoming a preferred choice for developers who value strong typing, .NET integration, and the ability to reuse existing code and libraries.

This book aims to elevate your Blazor development skills by focusing on the creation of advanced UI components. Understanding how to design and implement these components is crucial for building applications that are not only scalable but also maintainable over the long term. By mastering these techniques, you will be able to create complex, reusable components that enhance the functionality and user experience of your Blazor applications.

Target Audience

This book is intended for experienced Blazor developers who are eager to deepen their understanding of component design and customization. Whether you're looking to refine your skills or explore the full range of Blazor's capabilities, this book will guide you through advanced concepts that go beyond the basics.

Additionally, this book serves developers transitioning from other frameworks, such as Angular, React, or Vue, who want to leverage their existing knowledge while gaining advanced insights into Blazor's unique features and architecture. If you're familiar with frontend development but new to Blazor, this book will help you quickly bridge the gap and apply your skills effectively in the Blazor ecosystem.

How to Use This Book

The book is structured to progressively build your knowledge and expertise in advanced Blazor component development. Each chapter delves into specific topics, starting with foundational concepts and moving towards more complex, real-world scenarios. You'll find practical examples and detailed explanations that will help you apply the lessons to your projects.

To get the most out of this book, it's assumed that you have a solid understanding of Blazor basics, C#, and general web development concepts. If you're already comfortable with creating basic Blazor applications, this book will help you push the boundaries of what you can achieve with advanced component techniques. Whether you're working on a personal project or in a professional environment, the knowledge gained from this book will empower you to build sophisticated, high-performance Blazor applications.

Chapter 1: Understanding Blazor's Component Model

Blazor's component model is the foundation upon which the framework is built, providing a robust architecture for creating interactive, dynamic web applications. In this chapter, we will explore the core principles that govern Blazor components, from their lifecycle to their rendering process. By understanding how components work under the hood, you'll gain insights into how to leverage them effectively in your applications. This knowledge is crucial for anyone looking to master Blazor and build applications that are both efficient and easy to maintain. As we dive into the details, you'll see how Blazor's component model not only simplifies development but also offers the flexibility needed to create complex, reusable UI elements.

Revisiting the Basics: Components, Razor Syntax, and the Lifecycle

At the heart of Blazor lies its component-based architecture, which allows developers to break down the user interface into smaller, reusable pieces. A Blazor component is essentially a self-contained unit of UI that includes the HTML markup and the logic required to render and manage it. These components can be composed together to build complex UIs in a modular fashion.

Blazor components are typically written using Razor syntax, a combination of HTML and C#. Razor allows you to seamlessly integrate C# logic within your markup, making it easy to create dynamic web applications. For instance, you can use @ directives to embed C# expressions directly into your HTML, enabling real-time updates and interaction.

Understanding the lifecycle of a Blazor component is essential for effective development. The lifecycle consists of several stages, including initialization (`OnInitialized`), parameter setting (`OnParametersSet`), and rendering (`OnAfterRender`). Each of these stages offers hooks where you can execute custom logic, giving you fine-grained control over how your components behave throughout their lifecycle.

Advantages of Blazor's Component-Based Architecture in Building Complex UIs

Blazor's component-based architecture provides several significant advantages when building complex user interfaces. One of the primary benefits is reusability. By encapsulating UI logic and structure within components, you can reuse these components across different parts of your application, or even in different projects. This reduces code duplication and makes your applications easier to maintain.

Another advantage is the modularity it offers. By breaking down your application into smaller components, you can manage and develop each piece independently, which leads to better organization and a clearer separation of concerns. This modularity also enhances testability, as each component can be tested in isolation, ensuring that individual pieces function correctly before they are integrated into the larger application.

Blazor's architecture also promotes consistency in the UI. Since components can be reused and shared, you can maintain a consistent look and feel across your application. Changes to a single component can propagate throughout the application, ensuring that updates are uniform and reducing the chances of inconsistencies.

Blazor components can be easily nested and composed, allowing developers to build sophisticated and complex UIs by assembling simpler building blocks. This compositional approach is particularly powerful in scenarios where UI complexity grows, as it keeps the codebase manageable and scalable.

Blazor's component architecture not only simplifies the process of building and maintaining complex UIs but also offers the flexibility and power needed to create modern, scalable web applications. By revisiting the fundamentals and understanding the benefits, you'll be better equipped to harness the full potential of Blazor in your projects.

Cascading Parameters, Event Callbacks, and Managing State Across Components

As you progress in Blazor development, understanding and utilizing advanced component parameters becomes essential for building more sophisticated and dynamic applications. These advanced features enable components to interact with each other in more flexible and powerful ways, allowing you to create complex UIs that are both responsive and maintainable.

Cascading Parameters are one such feature that allow you to pass data down a component hierarchy without the need for explicitly defining parameters at each level. This is particularly useful when you have data or services that need to be accessed by multiple nested components. For instance, you might have a theme setting or a user authentication state that should be accessible to several components in the tree. By using the `CascadingParameter` attribute, you can efficiently share this data across multiple components, reducing boilerplate code and simplifying your component structure.

Event Callbacks play a crucial role in enabling child components to communicate with their parent components. Using the `EventCallback<T>` type, you can define events in child components that trigger actions in the parent. This is particularly useful for handling user interactions, such as button clicks or form submissions, where the parent component needs to react to changes in the child component. Event callbacks not only support the passing of data from child to parent but also allow for asynchronous event handling, ensuring that your application remains responsive even during complex operations.

Managing State Across Components is another critical aspect of building complex Blazor applications. In scenarios where multiple components need to share and update the same data, state management becomes a key concern. Blazor provides several approaches to manage state, including using shared services, cascading parameters, or dedicated state management libraries. By maintaining a centralized state that components can observe and react to, you can ensure that your application behaves consistently, with all parts of the UI reflecting the current state of the application. This becomes particularly important in scenarios involving user authentication, global settings, or other shared data.

Use Cases for Dynamic Component Rendering and the Importance of Lifecycle Methods

Dynamic Component Rendering is a powerful feature in Blazor that allows you to render components at runtime based on dynamic conditions. This capability is particularly useful in scenarios where the components to be displayed are not known until runtime, such as in a dashboard application where the displayed widgets can be configured by the user. Blazor's `DynamicComponent` feature allows you to instantiate components based on their type, passing parameters dynamically and managing their state as needed.

For example, you might have a component that renders different types of charts depending on the data being visualized. By leveraging dynamic component rendering, you can switch between different chart components based on user input or other conditions without hardcoding each possible option into your UI.

Lifecycle Methods play a critical role when dealing with dynamic components or any scenario where the component's state and behavior need to be carefully managed. These methods, such as `OnInitialized`, `OnParametersSet`, and `OnAfterRender`, provide hooks into key moments in a component's lifecycle, allowing you to initialize data, react to parameter changes, or perform cleanup operations. Understanding when and how to use these lifecycle methods is crucial for ensuring that your components behave correctly, especially when dealing with complex state management, asynchronous operations, or dynamic rendering.

For instance, when rendering a dynamic component, you might need to fetch data asynchronously before the component is fully rendered. In this case, you can use the `OnInitializedAsync` method to load the necessary data, ensuring that the component only renders once all the required data is available. Similarly, the `OnAfterRenderAsync` method can be used to trigger additional logic after the component has rendered, such as initializing a JavaScript interop operation or performing a UI update that depends on the final rendered state.

Mastering advanced component parameters and understanding the intricacies of dynamic component rendering and lifecycle methods are essential skills for any Blazor developer aiming to build complex and responsive applications. These techniques not only enhance the flexibility and power of your components but also ensure that your application remains maintainable and scalable as it grows in complexity.

Structuring Components for Reusability and Maintainability

Creating reusable and maintainable components is one of the key strengths of Blazor, enabling you to build scalable applications efficiently. To maximize reusability, it's important to design components with a clear separation of concerns and minimal coupling. Here are some best practices to follow:

1. **Single Responsibility Principle (SRP):** Each component should have a single, well-defined responsibility. This not only makes the component easier to understand and test but also enhances its reusability in different contexts. For instance, a button component should focus solely on rendering a button and handling its click event, without taking on responsibilities like data fetching or state management, which should be handled by other components or services.

2. **Parameterization:** Design your components to be flexible and adaptable by making extensive use of parameters. Parameters allow you to customize the behavior and appearance of a component without modifying its internal logic. For example, a `Card` component can be parameterized with properties like `Title`, `Content`, and `Footer`, enabling it to be

used in various parts of your application with different content.

3. **Encapsulation:** Keep the internal implementation details of a component hidden from other parts of the application. By encapsulating the component's logic and state, you ensure that changes within the component do not inadvertently affect other components or the application as a whole. Use private fields or methods within your component to protect its internal state, exposing only the necessary public parameters or events.

4. **Avoiding Hardcoded Dependencies:** Reusable components should avoid hardcoding dependencies like services or configuration values. Instead, inject these dependencies through constructor injection or use cascading parameters where appropriate. This makes the component more adaptable and easier to integrate into different parts of your application or even into different projects.

5. **Consistent Naming Conventions:** Use consistent and descriptive naming conventions for your components and their parameters. This improves readability and helps other developers understand the purpose and usage of each component quickly. For instance, prefixing reusable UI components with a common identifier like `App` (e.g., `AppButton`, `AppCard`) can help in organizing and identifying components that are shared across your application.

Techniques for Breaking Down Complex UIs into Manageable Components

When building complex user interfaces, it's essential to break down the UI into smaller, manageable components. This modular approach not only simplifies development but also makes the UI easier to maintain and extend over time.

Here are some strategies for effectively breaking down complex UIs:

1. **Top-Down Decomposition:** Start by designing the high-level layout of your application. Identify the major sections of the UI, such as headers, footers, sidebars, and main content areas. Each of these sections can then be broken down into smaller components. For example, a sidebar might contain a navigation menu component, which in turn contains individual navigation link components.

2. **Component Composition:** Leverage component composition to build complex UIs from simpler building blocks. For example, a `Dashboard` component might be composed of several `Widget` components, each responsible for displaying a different piece of information. By composing these widgets within the dashboard, you create a modular and flexible UI that can easily be modified by adding, removing, or rearranging the widgets.

3. **Functional Grouping:** Group related UI elements into components based on their functionality. For instance, if your application has a form with multiple input fields, consider grouping these fields into a `FormField` component that handles common tasks like validation and error display. This not only reduces code duplication but also makes it easier to manage changes, as updates to the `FormField` component will automatically propagate to all forms that use it.

4. **Presentational vs. Container Components:** Differentiate between presentational components, which focus on rendering UI, and container components, which handle data fetching and state management. Presentational components should be purely concerned with displaying data and should

receive all necessary data via parameters. Container components, on the other hand, manage the state and pass data down to presentational components. This separation of concerns helps in keeping your components clean and focused on their specific roles.

5. **Iterative Refinement:** As you develop your application, iteratively refine your components by extracting subcomponents from larger components whenever you notice repeated patterns or complex logic. For example, if you find that multiple pages use a similar layout or structure, consider extracting this common layout into a reusable `PageLayout` component. This iterative process helps in gradually building a robust and modular component library.

Adhering to these best practices for reusability and modularity can create Blazor components that are not only easy to reuse across your application but also easier to maintain and extend as your application grows. This approach will lead to a more organized, efficient, and scalable codebase, allowing you to build sophisticated UIs with confidence and ease.

Chapter 2: Building Customizable UI Components

Customizable UI components are the cornerstone of creating versatile and dynamic applications in Blazor. In this chapter, we will explore the process of designing and building components that can be easily customized and reused across various parts of your application. From defining flexible parameters to implementing advanced styling options, you'll learn how to create components that adapt to different contexts while maintaining a consistent look and feel. By mastering the techniques covered in this chapter, you'll be equipped to build UI elements that not only meet the immediate needs of your project but also scale and evolve with your application over time.

Defining the Goals and Requirements of Highly Customizable Components

Highly customizable components are essential for creating versatile user interfaces that can be adapted to various contexts and requirements. The primary goal of such components is to provide a high degree of flexibility without sacrificing usability or performance. This flexibility allows developers to tailor the appearance and behavior of components according to specific use cases, ensuring that they fit seamlessly into different parts of an application or even across multiple projects.

To achieve this, customizable components should be designed with the following key requirements in mind:

1. **Parameterization:** Customizable components should expose parameters that allow developers to configure key aspects of their appearance and

behavior. These parameters might include properties such as colors, sizes, content, and event handlers. By offering a well-defined set of parameters, components can be easily adjusted to meet the needs of different scenarios without requiring code changes within the component itself.

2. **Styling Options:** Components should support flexible styling options to allow developers to apply custom CSS or other styling mechanisms. This might include the ability to pass in CSS classes, style attributes, or even support for theming. Proper styling capabilities ensure that components can be integrated into various design systems and visual themes.

3. **Extensibility:** A highly customizable component should be designed to accommodate extensions or modifications without needing to rewrite the core component. This can be achieved through patterns like composition, where smaller components are combined to form more complex ones, or through the use of slots and templates that allow developers to inject custom content or behavior into the component.

4. **Consistency:** Even with high levels of customization, it's crucial that components maintain consistency in their usage patterns and interfaces. This consistency ensures that developers can predictably and reliably use components across different parts of an application, reducing the learning curve and potential for errors.

5. **Documentation and Examples:** Customizable components should be well-documented, with clear examples demonstrating how to use them in different scenarios. This helps developers quickly understand how to leverage the component's flexibility and apply it effectively in their projects.

Balancing Flexibility with Complexity: When to Abstract and When to Specialize

While flexibility is a key feature of customizable components, it's important to balance this flexibility with the complexity that it introduces. The more customizable a component is, the more complex it can become to understand and use effectively. Therefore, it's crucial to carefully consider when to abstract functionality into a highly flexible component and when to specialize components for specific use cases.

When to Abstract:

- **Reusability Across Multiple Contexts:** If a component is likely to be used in various parts of the application or across different projects, it's worth abstracting common functionality into a customizable component. For example, a `Button` component that can be styled, sized, and configured with different icons or behaviors would be a good candidate for abstraction because buttons are used widely in many interfaces.
- **Shared Business Logic:** When multiple parts of an application share the same logic but display it differently, abstracting that logic into a customizable component can reduce code duplication and centralize maintenance. For instance, a `Notification` component that handles alert messages with various display styles (e.g., success, warning, error) should be abstracted to allow different uses while maintaining consistent behavior.
- **Ease of Maintenance:** Abstracting commonly used functionality into a single customizable component can simplify maintenance. Updates or bug fixes

applied to the component automatically benefit all areas of the application that use it, ensuring consistency and reducing the effort required to make widespread changes.

When to Specialize:

- **Simplicity and Performance:** If a component is only used in a specific context or has performance-critical requirements, it may be better to specialize rather than abstract. Specialization can reduce the overhead of supporting unnecessary customization options and ensure the component is optimized for its intended use.
- **Minimizing Cognitive Load:** Highly abstract components can become difficult to configure and understand, especially for new developers or those unfamiliar with the project. In cases where a component is complex or has many configuration options, it may be more practical to create specialized components that are simpler to use and understand.
- **Specific Design Requirements:** When a component must adhere to very specific design or behavior requirements that are unlikely to be reused elsewhere, specialization makes sense. For example, a custom `Header` component designed to match a unique branding guideline may be better off as a specialized component rather than a generic, customizable one.

The decision to abstract or specialize components depends on the specific needs of your application. By carefully balancing flexibility with complexity, you can create components that are both powerful and easy to use, providing the right level of customization without overwhelming developers or compromising performance. This balance is key to building a maintainable, scalable Blazor application that can grow and evolve over time.

Implementing Render Fragments for Customizable Templates

Render fragments are a powerful feature in Blazor that allow developers to create customizable and dynamic templates within components. A render fragment is a block of UI that can be passed as a parameter to a component, giving developers the flexibility to define custom content within the context of the component. This makes it possible to build highly adaptable components where the structure and content can be customized without altering the component's internal logic.

To implement a render fragment, you define a `RenderFragment` parameter in your component. This parameter can then be used within the component's Razor markup to insert custom content. For example, consider a `Card` component where the header, body, and footer content can be customized using render fragments:

```
<!-- Card.razor -->
<div class="card">
    <div class="card-header">
        @HeaderContent
    </div>
    <div class="card-body">
        @BodyContent
    </div>
    <div class="card-footer">
        @FooterContent
    </div>
</div>

@code {
```

```
    [Parameter]
    public RenderFragment? HeaderContent { get;
set; }

    [Parameter]
    public RenderFragment? BodyContent { get;
set; }

    [Parameter]
    public RenderFragment? FooterContent { get;
set; }
}
```

In this example, the Card component defines three render fragments: HeaderContent, BodyContent, and FooterContent. These fragments allow the consumer of the Card component to provide custom content for each section:

```
<!-- Usage of Card component -->
<Card>
    <HeaderContent>
        <h3>Card Title</h3>
    </HeaderContent>
    <BodyContent>
        <p>This is the main content of the
card.</p>
    </BodyContent>
    <FooterContent>
        <button class="btn btn-
primary">Action</button>
    </FooterContent>
</Card>
```

Here, the custom content defined inside HeaderContent, BodyContent, and FooterContent is passed to the Card component, allowing for complete control over what is displayed in each section. This level of customization is essential for building components that can adapt to different use cases while maintaining a consistent structure.

Child Content and Named Templates for Enhancing Component Flexibility

Child content is a specific type of render fragment that allows you to define the main content of a component directly within its tags. Blazor supports this through the `[Parameter]` attribute, using a special parameter named `ChildContent` by convention. This is particularly useful for components that act as containers for other content, such as layout components, lists, or wrappers.

For example, consider a `Panel` component that uses child content to display whatever content is placed inside its tags:

```
<!-- Panel.razor -->
<div class="panel">
    <h2>@Title</h2>
    <div class="panel-body">
        @ChildContent
    </div>
</div>

@code {
    [Parameter]
    public string Title { get; set; } =
string.Empty;

    [Parameter]
    public RenderFragment? ChildContent { get;
set; }
}
```

The `Panel` component above can be used like this:

```
<!-- Usage of Panel component -->
<Panel Title="Panel Title">
    <p>This is the panel's body content.</p>
</Panel>
```

The content inside the `Panel` tags is rendered in the location defined by the `@ChildContent` parameter, making it simple to pass arbitrary content into the component.

Named Templates are an extension of this concept, allowing you to define multiple render fragments with specific names, enhancing the flexibility of your components. This is useful when a component has multiple areas where custom content can be inserted, each serving a different purpose.

Consider a `Table` component that supports custom content for its header, body, and footer using named templates:

```
<!-- Table.razor -->
<table class="table">
    <thead>
        @HeaderTemplate
    </thead>
    <tbody>
        @BodyTemplate
    </tbody>
    <tfoot>
        @FooterTemplate
    </tfoot>
</table>

@code {
    [Parameter]
    public RenderFragment? HeaderTemplate
{ get; set; }

    [Parameter]
    public RenderFragment? BodyTemplate { get;
set; }

    [Parameter]
    public RenderFragment? FooterTemplate
{ get; set; }
}
```

This `Table` component can be utilized with custom content provided for each named template:

```
<!-- Usage of Table component -->
<Table>
    <HeaderTemplate>
        <tr>
            <th>Name</th>
            <th>Age</th>
        </tr>
    </HeaderTemplate>
    <BodyTemplate>
        <tr>
            <td>John Doe</td>
            <td>30</td>
        </tr>
        <tr>
            <td>Jane Smith</td>
            <td>28</td>
        </tr>
    </BodyTemplate>
    <FooterTemplate>
        <tr>
            <td colspan="2">Footer Content
Here</td>
        </tr>
    </FooterTemplate>
</Table>
```

In this example, the `Table` component receives three different render fragments, each corresponding to a specific section of the table (`HeaderTemplate`, `BodyTemplate`, and `FooterTemplate`). This approach provides a high degree of customization, allowing the `Table` component to be used in a variety of contexts without needing to alter its internal implementation.

Using render fragments and child content in Blazor allows you to build highly customizable components that can adapt to a wide range of scenarios. By leveraging these techniques, you can create components that offer flexibility and reuse, making your Blazor applications more modular, maintainable, and scalable. Named templates further extend this flexibility, enabling you to define distinct customizable sections within your components, thereby enhancing their versatility and power.

Techniques for Dynamic Component Generation Based on Runtime Data

In Blazor, dynamically generating components based on runtime data is a powerful technique that enables you to create flexible, data-driven user interfaces. This approach is particularly useful when the structure or content of your UI cannot be determined at compile time but rather depends on user input, configuration settings, or other dynamic data sources.

One of the primary tools for dynamic component generation in Blazor is the `DynamicComponent` component, which allows you to render components based on their type at runtime. Here's an example scenario where you might want to render different components depending on the type of data being processed:

```
@page "/DynamicSample"

@using
AdvanceBlazorBookCompanionCode.Components.Contr
ols
@using Microsoft.AspNetCore.Components

<!-- DynamicComponentDemo.razor -->
@foreach (var componentType in componentTypes)
{
    var parametersForComponent =
GetParametersForComponent(componentType);
```

```razor
    <DynamicComponent Type="@componentType"
Parameters="@parametersForComponent" />
}

@code {
    private List<Type> componentTypes = new
List<Type>
    {
        typeof(TextComponent),
        typeof(ImageComponent),
        typeof(ButtonComponent)
    };

    private Dictionary<string, object>
parameters = new Dictionary<string, object>
    {
        { "Text", "Dynamic content here" },
        { "ImageUrl", "example.jpg" },
        { "ButtonLabel", "Click Me" }
    };

    private Dictionary<string, object>
GetParametersForComponent(Type componentType)
    {
        if (componentType ==
typeof(TextComponent))
        {
            return new Dictionary<string,
object>
            {
                { "Text", "Dynamic content
here" }
            };
        }
        else if (componentType ==
typeof(ImageComponent))
        {
            return new Dictionary<string,
object>
            {
                { "ImageUrl", "example.jpg" }
            };
        }
```

```
        else if (componentType ==
typeof(ButtonComponent))
        {
            return new Dictionary<string,
object>
            {
                { "ButtonLabel", "Click Me" }
            };
        }
        else
        {
            return new Dictionary<string,
object>();
        }
    }
}
```

In this example, the `DynamicComponent` renders different components (`TextComponent`, `ImageComponent`, and `ButtonComponent`) based on the list of types provided in `componentTypes`. The `Parameters` property is used to pass parameters dynamically to each component, allowing for further customization.

This technique is especially useful in scenarios such as:

- **Dynamic Dashboards:** Where widgets are rendered based on user preferences or configurations.
- **Form Builders:** Where different input types (textboxes, dropdowns, checkboxes) are rendered based on form definitions stored in a database.
- **Content Management Systems (CMS):** Where content blocks of various types (text, images, videos) need to be dynamically rendered on a page.

Another approach for dynamic content rendering is using conditional logic within Razor templates. For instance, you can use `@if`, `@else`, and `@switch` statements to

conditionally render components based on the runtime
state:

```razor
<!-- ConditionalComponentRendering.razor -->
@switch (contentType)
{
    case "text":
        <TextComponent Text="This is a text
component" />
        break;
    case "image":
        <ImageComponent ImageUrl="example.png"
/>
        break;
    case "button":
        <ButtonComponent ButtonLabel="Click Me"
/>
        break;
}
```

In this example, different components are rendered based
on the value of the contentType variable, allowing you to
tailor the UI to the specific needs of the application at
runtime.

Best Practices for Performance Optimization
When Rendering Complex UIs

When dynamically rendering components, especially in
scenarios involving complex UIs or large datasets,
performance optimization becomes a critical concern. Here
are some best practices to ensure that your Blazor
application remains responsive and efficient:

1. **Lazy Loading of Components:** For complex UIs
   that include many components or data-intensive
   operations, consider lazy loading components only
   when they are needed. This can be achieved by

conditionally rendering components based on user interactions or scroll events. By deferring the loading of non-critical components, you can reduce the initial load time and improve the perceived performance of your application.

```
<!-- LazyLoadingComponent.razor -->
@if (loadComponent)
{
    <HeavyComponent />
}

<button @onclick="() => loadComponent =
true">Load Component</button>

@code {
    private bool loadComponent = false;
}
```

2. **Virtualization:** For rendering large lists or grids, use Blazor's built-in virtualization feature. Virtualization renders only the visible items within a list, drastically reducing the number of DOM elements and improving performance. This technique is particularly useful for scenarios like infinite scrolling or paginated data grids.

```
<Virtualize Items="@items" ItemSize="50">
    <ItemContent>
        @(context => <div>@context</div>)
    </ItemContent>
</Virtualize>

@code {
    private List<string> items =
Enumerable.Range(1, 10000).Select(i =>
$"Item {i}").ToList();
}
```

In this example, the `Virtualize` component ensures that only the visible items in the `items` list are rendered, which optimizes both memory usage and rendering performance.

3. **Efficient State Management:** Managing state effectively is key to optimizing performance in dynamic UIs. Avoid unnecessary re-renders by ensuring that state changes are localized to the components that truly need to update. This can be done by using Blazor's `ShouldRender` method, which allows you to control when a component should re-render.

```
@code {
    protected override bool
ShouldRender()
    {
        // Only render if specific
conditions are met
        return someCondition;
    }
}
```

This method can prevent costly re-renders and ensure that only the components affected by a state change are updated.

4. **Batching and Throttling Updates:** When dealing with frequent state updates or UI interactions, consider batching or throttling updates to reduce the rendering load. Instead of updating the UI immediately on every interaction, you can batch updates and apply them at intervals, reducing the number of re-renders and improving performance.

```
private async Task ThrottleUpdates()
{
```

```
    // Throttle UI updates to once per
100ms
    await Task.Delay(100);
    StateHasChanged();
}
```

5. **Minimizing DOM Interactions:** Minimize direct DOM manipulations, as these can be expensive in terms of performance. Instead, rely on Blazor's data binding and event handling mechanisms, which are optimized for performance. If DOM interactions are necessary, such as when integrating with JavaScript libraries, use Blazor's JavaScript interop judiciously and ensure that these operations are as efficient as possible.

Dynamically rendering components based on runtime data offers significant flexibility in building adaptable and interactive UIs. However, it's important to balance this flexibility with careful performance considerations. By following best practices such as lazy loading, virtualization, efficient state management, and minimizing DOM interactions, you can ensure that your Blazor application remains performant even as its complexity grows. These techniques will help you create rich, dynamic interfaces that respond efficiently to user interactions and data changes.

Chapter 3: Advanced State Management within Components

Effective state management is crucial for building dynamic and responsive Blazor applications. As applications grow in complexity, managing state across components becomes increasingly challenging. In this chapter, we will delve into advanced techniques for managing state within Blazor components, exploring strategies that go beyond basic state handling. You'll learn how to implement patterns that ensure data consistency, optimize performance, and maintain a clear separation of concerns. Whether you're dealing with local component state, shared state across multiple components, or global application state, this chapter will provide you with the tools and insights needed to master state management in Blazor.

Overview of State Management Options: Local Component State, Cascading State, and Global State

Effective state management is key to building responsive and maintainable Blazor applications, particularly as the complexity of your UI increases. In Blazor, state can be managed at different levels depending on the scope and sharing requirements of the data. Understanding when and how to use these different state management options is essential for creating scalable and efficient applications.

Local Component State:
Local component state is the simplest form of state management in Blazor. It refers to the state that is maintained within a single component and is not shared with other components. This state is typically managed

using properties or fields within the component's `@code` block. Local state is ideal for simple, isolated scenarios where the state does not need to be accessed or modified by other components.

For example, a form component might manage the state of its input fields locally:

```razor
<!-- LoginForm.razor -->
<EditForm Model="loginModel"
OnValidSubmit="HandleLogin">
    <InputText @bind-
Value="loginModel.Username" placeholder="Enter
user name" />
    <InputText @bind-
Value="loginModel.Password" placeholder="Enter
password" type="password" /></EditForm>

@code {
    private LoginModel loginModel = new
LoginModel();

    private void HandleLogin()
    {
        // Handle login logic here
    }

    private class LoginModel
    {
        public string Username { get; set; }
        public string Password { get; set; }
    }
}
```

In this example, `loginModel` is a local state that holds the form data and is managed entirely within the `LoginForm` component.

Cascading State:
Cascading state allows state to be shared across a hierarchy

of components without needing to pass it explicitly through each component in the tree. This is particularly useful when multiple components need to access the same state, such as a theme or authentication context.

Cascading values are provided by using the CascadingValue component, which makes the state available to all descendants:

```
<!-- App.razor -->
<CascadingValue Value="currentUser">
    <MainLayout />
</CascadingValue>

@code {
    private User currentUser = new User { Name
= "John Doe", IsAuthenticated = true };
}

<!-- MainLayout.razor -->
@code {
    [CascadingParameter]
    public User CurrentUser { get; set; } =
default!;
}

<div>
    Welcome, @CurrentUser.Name
</div>
```

Here, the currentUser state is shared with all components within the MainLayout component and any of its descendants. This approach simplifies state sharing and ensures consistency across the UI.

Global State:
Global state refers to state that is accessible throughout the entire application. This is typically managed using a shared service or state container that is registered in the

dependency injection (DI) container and injected into components as needed. Global state is ideal for managing data that must be consistently available across different parts of the application, such as user authentication data, application settings, or global notifications.

A simple example of a global state container might look like this:

```
<!-- AppState.cs -->
public class AppState
{
    public string Theme { get; set; } =
"Light";

    public event Action? OnChange;

    public void SetTheme(string theme)
    {
        Theme = theme;
        NotifyStateChanged();
    }

    private void NotifyStateChanged() =>
OnChange?.Invoke();
}

<!-- Registration in Program.cs -->
builder.Services.AddSingleton<AppState>();

<!-- Component using AppState -->
@inject AppState appState

<button @onclick="ToggleTheme">Toggle
Theme</button>
<p>Current Theme: @appState.Theme</p>

@code {
    private void ToggleTheme()
    {
        var newTheme = appState.Theme ==
"Light" ? "Dark" : "Light";
```

```
            appState.SetTheme(newTheme);
    }
}
```

In this example, `AppState` is a global state container managing the application's theme. Any component can access and modify the theme via dependency injection, and all components will reflect the updated state.

Patterns for Managing State in Complex UIs (e.g., MVU, Flux)

As your application grows in complexity, more structured patterns for state management become necessary to maintain clarity and ensure that your UI remains responsive and maintainable. Two popular patterns for managing state in complex UIs are Model-View-Update (MVU) and Flux.

Model-View-Update (MVU):

The MVU pattern is particularly well-suited for functional programming and is inspired by the Elm architecture. In the context of Blazor, MVU involves structuring your components around three key concepts:

- **Model:** The immutable state of your UI.
- **View:** The UI representation, derived from the model.
- **Update:** The function that produces a new model based on the current model and an action (event).

In Blazor, you can implement MVU by organizing your state and event handling logic in a way that aligns with this pattern:

```
<!-- CounterComponent.razor -->
@code {
    private int count = 0;
```

```csharp
    private void Increment()
    {
        count++;
    }

    private void Decrement()
    {
        count--;
    }

    private RenderFragment View() => builder =>
    {
        builder.OpenElement(0, "div");
        builder.AddContent(1, $"Current count:
{count}");
        builder.CloseElement();

        builder.OpenElement(2, "button");
        builder.AddAttribute(3, "onclick",
EventCallback.Factory.Create(this, Increment));
        builder.AddContent(4, "Increment");
        builder.CloseElement();

        builder.OpenElement(5, "button");
        builder.AddAttribute(6, "onclick",
EventCallback.Factory.Create(this, Decrement));
        builder.AddContent(7, "Decrement");
        builder.CloseElement();
    };

    protected override void
BuildRenderTree(RenderTreeBuilder builder)
    {
        builder.AddContent(0, View());
    }
}
```

Here, the state (count) and UI are tightly linked, with
changes in the state (model) triggering an update to the UI
(view).

Flux Pattern:

The Flux pattern, popularized by Facebook, is another powerful pattern for managing state, especially in applications with complex data flows. Flux introduces the concept of a unidirectional data flow, where actions trigger state changes in a central store, and the UI reacts to these changes.

The key components of Flux are:

- **Action:** A payload of information that triggers a state change.
- **Dispatcher:** The central hub that receives actions and dispatches them to the store.
- **Store:** The centralized state container that holds and manages the application state.
- **View:** The UI components that subscribe to the store and update when the state changes.

While Blazor doesn't have a built-in Flux implementation, you can create your own or use third-party libraries to implement this pattern. Here's a simple example:

```
<!-- Action.cs -->
public class Action
{
    public string Type { get; }
    public object? Payload { get; }

    public Action(string type, object? payload = null)
    {
        Type = type;
        Payload = payload;
    }
}

<!-- Store.cs -->
public class Store
```

```csharp
{
    private readonly List<Action> _actions =
new List<Action>();
    public string State { get; private set; } =
"Initial State";

    public event Action? OnChange;

    public void Dispatch(Action action)
    {
        _actions.Add(action);
        Reduce(action);
        NotifyStateChanged();
    }

    private void Reduce(Action action)
    {
        switch (action.Type)
        {
            case "SET_STATE":
                State =
action.Payload?.ToString() ?? State;
                break;
            // Handle other actions
        }
    }

    private void NotifyStateChanged() =>
OnChange?.Invoke();
}

<!-- Registration in Program.cs -->
builder.Services.AddSingleton<Store>();

<!-- Component using Store -->
@inject Store store

<button @onclick="() => store.Dispatch(new
Action("SET_STATE", "New State"))">Change
State</button>
<p>Current State: @store.State</p>

@code {
    protected override void OnInitialized()
```

```
    {
        store.OnChange += StateHasChanged;
    }

    public void Dispose()
    {
        store.OnChange -= StateHasChanged;
    }
}
```

This simple Flux-like implementation allows components to dispatch actions to a central store, which then updates its state and notifies all subscribers of the change. The unidirectional flow of data helps to prevent common issues such as inconsistent state or data corruption, making it easier to manage complex interactions within your UI.

State management in Blazor can range from straightforward local state handling to more sophisticated patterns like MVU and Flux for complex UIs. By selecting the appropriate state management strategy for your application's needs, you can ensure that your Blazor applications remain maintainable, scalable, and responsive. Whether using local, cascading, or global state, or adopting advanced patterns like MVU and Flux, the key is to maintain a clear and consistent approach to managing the state across your components.

Techniques for Synchronizing State Across Components

As applications grow in complexity, the need to synchronize state across multiple components becomes more critical. State synchronization ensures that all parts of the UI reflect the current state of the application, providing a consistent user experience. Blazor offers several techniques to achieve state synchronization across components.

1. **Using Cascading Parameters:** Cascading parameters, as discussed earlier, are a powerful way to share state across a component hierarchy. When you use a cascading value, any descendant component can access and update that value, ensuring that all dependent components stay in sync. This method is ideal for scenarios where the state needs to be shared across a set of related components.

   ```
   <!-- ParentComponent.razor -->
   <CascadingValue Value="sharedState">
       <ChildComponent />
   </CascadingValue>

   @code {
       private string sharedState = "Initial
   State";
   }

   <!-- ChildComponent.razor -->
   @code {
       [CascadingParameter]
       public string SharedState { get;
   set; } = string.Empty;

       private void UpdateState()
       {
           SharedState = "Updated State";
       }
   }
   ```

   In this example, `ChildComponent` receives and can modify `sharedState`, ensuring that any changes are reflected across all components that use this state.

2. **Event Callbacks for State Propagation:** For cases
   where child components need to notify parent
   components of state changes, event callbacks are an
   effective tool. This approach allows child
   components to trigger updates in their parents,
   ensuring that state changes are propagated correctly.

```
<!-- ParentComponent.razor -->
<ChildComponent
OnStateChanged="HandleStateChanged" />

@code {
    private string parentState = "Initial
State";

    private void
HandleStateChanged(string newState)
    {
        parentState = newState;
    }
}

<!-- ChildComponent.razor -->
@code {
    [Parameter]
    public EventCallback<string>
OnStateChanged { get; set; }

    private void NotifyParent()
    {
        OnStateChanged.InvokeAsync("New
State from Child");
    }
}
```

Here, ChildComponent can notify
ParentComponent of state changes, allowing the
parent to update its own state accordingly.

3. **Shared Services for Global State:** For more
   complex scenarios where state needs to be

synchronized across unrelated components or throughout the entire application, shared services are an effective solution. A service registered in the dependency injection container can act as a central state manager, allowing any component to access and modify the state.

```csharp
// AppState.cs
public class AppState
{
    private string _sharedState =
"Initial State";

    public string SharedState
    {
        get => _sharedState;
        set
        {
            if (_sharedState != value)
            {
                _sharedState = value;
                NotifyStateChanged();
            }
        }
    }

    public event Action? OnChange;

    private void NotifyStateChanged() =>
OnChange?.Invoke();
}

// Registration in Program.cs
builder.Services.AddSingleton<AppState>()
;

// Using AppState in a component
@inject AppState appState

<p>@appState.SharedState</p>
```

```
<button @onclick="UpdateState">Update
State</button>

@code {
    private void UpdateState()
    {
        appState.SharedState = "Updated
State";
    }

    protected override void
OnInitialized()
    {
        appState.OnChange +=
StateHasChanged;
    }

    public void Dispose()
    {
        appState.OnChange -=
StateHasChanged;
    }
}
```

In this example, `AppState` manages shared state, and any component can subscribe to state changes to stay synchronized.

Implementing State Persistence Using Local Storage, Session Storage, and Server-Side Storage

State persistence is crucial for creating applications that maintain state across sessions or even after the application is closed. Blazor supports several mechanisms for persisting state, including local storage, session storage, and server-side storage.

1. **Local Storage:** Local storage is a client-side storage mechanism that allows you to store data that

persists even after the browser is closed. It is ideal for persisting user preferences, settings, or any other data that should survive browser sessions.

To use local storage in Blazor, you can leverage the `Microsoft.AspNetCore.Components.Web.Exten sions` package or implement JavaScript interop directly:

```
@inject IJSRuntime JS

<button @onclick="SaveState">Save
State</button>
<button @onclick="LoadState">Load
State</button>
<p>Stored State: @storedState</p>

@code {
    private string storedState = "Not
Loaded";

    private async Task SaveState()
    {
        await
JS.InvokeVoidAsync("localStorage.setItem"
, "appState", "My persisted state");
    }

    private async Task LoadState()
    {
        storedState = await
JS.InvokeAsync<string>("localStorage.getI
tem", "appState") ?? "No State";
    }
}
```

This example demonstrates saving and loading state to and from local storage. The stored data will be available even after the browser is closed and reopened.

2. **Session Storage:** Session storage works similarly to local storage but is scoped to the user's session. The data stored in session storage is only available for the duration of the page session and is cleared when the page session ends (e.g., when the browser is closed). Session storage is ideal for transient data that should not persist beyond the current session.

   The implementation is similar to local storage:

```
<button @onclick="SaveSessionState">Save
State to Session</button>
<button @onclick="LoadSessionState">Load
State from Session</button>
<p>Session State: @sessionState</p>

@code {
    private string sessionState = "Not
Loaded";

    private async Task SaveSessionState()
    {
        await
JS.InvokeVoidAsync("sessionStorage.setIte
m", "sessionState", "Session-based
state");
    }

    private async Task LoadSessionState()
    {
        sessionState = await
JS.InvokeAsync<string>("sessionStorage.ge
tItem", "sessionState") ?? "No State";
    }
}
```

3. **Server-Side Storage:** For more robust state persistence, especially when dealing with larger amounts of data or sensitive information, server-side storage is a preferred option. This can involve

storing state in a database, a distributed cache, or using ASP.NET Core's session state.

Server-side storage ensures that the state is maintained on the server and is not dependent on the client's browser. This approach is suitable for scenarios where you need to persist user data securely across devices or sessions.

```
// Server-side state management using
ASP.NET Core's session state
services.AddDistributedMemoryCache();
services.AddSession();

app.UseSession();

// Using session state in a controller
public IActionResult SaveState()
{

HttpContext.Session.SetString("MyState",
"Server persisted state");
    return Ok();
}

public IActionResult LoadState()
{
    var state =
HttpContext.Session.GetString("MyState")
?? "No State";
    return Ok(state);
}
```

In this example, state is stored on the server using session state, making it available across multiple requests within the same session.

Synchronizing and persisting state in Blazor requires a thoughtful approach depending on your application's needs. By leveraging techniques like cascading parameters, event callbacks, and shared services, you can ensure that your components remain synchronized and provide a consistent user experience. Additionally, by implementing state persistence using local storage, session storage, or server-side storage, you can maintain state across sessions, ensuring that your application's state is reliable and resilient. These strategies are essential for building robust Blazor applications that can handle complex state management scenarios effectively.

Minimizing Re-renders and Managing Expensive Computations

One of the key challenges in building responsive and performant Blazor applications is minimizing unnecessary re-renders and managing expensive computations effectively. Re-renders can degrade performance, particularly in applications with complex UIs or large amounts of data, making it crucial to understand how to optimize rendering behavior.

1. Use the `ShouldRender` Method:

Blazor's `ShouldRender` method provides a way to control whether a component should re-render in response to state changes. By overriding this method, you can prevent unnecessary re-renders, which is especially useful when dealing with components that don't need to update every time their parent or their own state changes.

```
@code {
    private bool shouldRender;

    protected override bool ShouldRender()
    {
        return shouldRender;
```

```
    }

    private void TriggerRender()
    {
        shouldRender = true;
        StateHasChanged();
    }
}
```

In this example, the component will only re-render when
shouldRender is set to true, allowing you to precisely
control when a re-render occurs.

2. Avoid Binding to Complex Expressions:

When binding data or events in Blazor, avoid binding
directly to complex expressions or methods that perform
expensive computations. Instead, pre-compute the value or
result in a local variable and bind to that variable. This
ensures that the computation only happens once, rather than
on every re-render.

```
@code {
    private string precomputedValue;

    protected override void OnInitialized()
    {
        precomputedValue =
ExpensiveComputation();
    }

    private string ExpensiveComputation()
    {
        // Simulate a complex operation
        return "Computed Value";
    }
}
```

3. Use `@key` Directive to Optimize List Rendering:

When rendering lists of items, Blazor reuses existing DOM elements to optimize rendering performance. However, this can sometimes lead to incorrect rendering if the items in the list change frequently. The `@key` directive helps Blazor correctly identify elements and minimize re-renders by assigning a unique key to each item.

```
@foreach (var item in items)
{
    <div @key="item.Id">@item.Name</div>
}
```

Using `@key` ensures that Blazor can efficiently manage the DOM elements, reducing the overhead of rendering lists.

4. Memorize Expensive Computations:

Memorization is a technique where you cache the results of expensive computations to avoid recalculating them unnecessarily. In Blazor, you can implement memorization by storing the result of a computation and reusing it as long as the inputs haven't changed.

```
@code {
    private Dictionary<int, string> cache =
new();

    private string GetExpensiveResult(int
input)
    {
        if (!cache.TryGetValue(input, out var
result))
        {
            result =
ExpensiveComputation(input);
            cache[input] = result;
```

```
        }
        return result;
    }

    private string ExpensiveComputation(int
input)
    {
        // Perform expensive calculation
        return $"Result for {input}";
    }
}
```

Techniques for Handling Large Datasets and High-Frequency Updates Efficiently

Blazor applications often need to handle large datasets or respond to high-frequency updates, such as real-time data streams. Without careful optimization, these scenarios can lead to performance bottlenecks. Here are some techniques to handle these challenges efficiently:

1. Virtualization for Large Datasets:

Virtualization is a powerful technique for rendering large datasets efficiently by only rendering the items that are currently visible on the screen. Blazor's `Virtualize` component makes it easy to implement virtualization in your applications.

```
<Virtualize Items="@largeDataSet"
ItemSize="50">
    <ItemContent>
        @(context => <div>@context</div>)
    </ItemContent>
</Virtualize>

@code {
    private List<string> largeDataSet =
Enumerable.Range(1, 10000).Select(i => $"Item
{i}").ToList();
```

}

In this example, only the visible items in `largeDataSet` are rendered, significantly reducing the rendering overhead and improving performance.

2. Throttling and Debouncing High-Frequency Events:

When dealing with high-frequency events, such as mouse movements or keypresses, it's important to throttle or debounce the event handlers to avoid overwhelming the UI with updates. Throttling ensures that the event handler is called at regular intervals, while debouncing ensures that it is only called after the event has stopped firing for a specified period.

```
@code {
    private System.Timers.Timer? debounceTimer;

    private void OnHighFrequencyEvent()
    {
        if (debounceTimer != null)
        {
            debounceTimer.Stop();
            debounceTimer.Dispose();
        }

        debounceTimer = new
System.Timers.Timer(200);
        debounceTimer.Elapsed += (s, e) =>
        {
            InvokeAsync(() => { /* Handle the
event */ });
            debounceTimer?.Dispose();
        };
        debounceTimer.Start();
    }
}
```

3. Lazy Loading of Data:

For large datasets, consider lazy loading or paging to reduce the amount of data loaded and rendered at once. This approach loads only a subset of the data initially and fetches more data as the user scrolls or interacts with the application.

```
@code {
    private List<string> items = new();
    private int loadedItemCount = 0;

    protected override async Task
OnInitializedAsync()
    {
        await LoadMoreItems();
    }

    private async Task LoadMoreItems()
    {
        // Simulate data loading
items.AddRange(Enumerable.Range(loadedItemCount
, 20).Select(i => $"Item {i}"));
        loadedItemCount += 20;
        StateHasChanged();
    }
}
```

4. Efficient Data Structures:

When handling large datasets, use efficient data structures that optimize for the operations you perform most frequently. For example, use `Dictionary` for fast lookups, `List` for ordered collections, and `HashSet` for ensuring uniqueness with quick access.

5. Background Processing for Expensive Operations:

For operations that are computationally expensive or time-consuming, consider offloading the work to a background task or service. This allows the UI to remain responsive while the heavy processing is done asynchronously.

```
@code {
    private async Task
HandleExpensiveOperation()
    {
        await Task.Run(() =>
        {
            // Perform expensive operation
        });
    }
}
```

Optimizing performance in Blazor requires a strategic approach to managing re-renders, computations, and data handling. By implementing techniques like ShouldRender, virtualization, throttling, and lazy loading, you can ensure that your Blazor applications remain responsive and efficient, even when dealing with complex UIs, large datasets, or high-frequency updates. These optimizations are key to delivering a smooth user experience and maintaining high performance in production environments.

Chapter 4: Implementing Design Patterns in Blazor Components

Design patterns are proven solutions to common problems in software development, offering structured approaches to writing clean, maintainable, and scalable code. In Blazor, applying these patterns to component design can significantly enhance the architecture of your applications, making them more robust and easier to manage as they grow in complexity. In this chapter, we will explore how to implement well-known design patterns within Blazor components, including patterns like MVVM (Model-View-ViewModel), Singleton, and Dependency Injection. By understanding and applying these patterns, you'll be able to build Blazor applications that are not only efficient and modular but also align with best practices in software engineering. Whether you are working on a small project or a large enterprise application, mastering these design patterns will equip you with the tools to tackle a wide range of development challenges effectively.

Overview of Common UI Design Patterns

Design patterns provide a blueprint for solving recurring problems in software design, helping developers structure their code in a way that is maintainable, flexible, and scalable. In the context of Blazor, certain design patterns can be particularly useful for building complex and reusable UI components. This section explores some of the most common UI design patterns—such as the Strategy Pattern, Factory Pattern, and Composite Pattern—and demonstrates how these can be applied effectively within the Blazor component model.

Strategy Pattern

The Strategy Pattern is a behavioral design pattern that
enables selecting an algorithm at runtime. Instead of
implementing multiple conditional statements to handle
different scenarios, the Strategy Pattern allows you to
encapsulate each algorithm in a separate class, and switch
between them easily.

Example in Blazor:

Imagine you are building a chart component that can render
different types of charts (e.g., line, bar, pie). Instead of
using if-else or switch statements to choose the rendering
logic, you can apply the Strategy Pattern.

```
// Define the strategy interface
public interface IChartStrategy
{
    RenderFragment RenderChart();
}

// Implement concrete strategies
public class LineChartStrategy : IChartStrategy
{
    public RenderFragment RenderChart() =>
builder =>
    {
        builder.AddContent(0, "Rendering a Line
Chart");
    };
}

public class BarChartStrategy : IChartStrategy
{
    public RenderFragment RenderChart() =>
builder =>
    {
```

```
         builder.AddContent(0, "Rendering a Bar
Chart");
     };
}

public class PieChartStrategy : IChartStrategy
{
    public RenderFragment RenderChart() =>
builder =>
    {
        builder.AddContent(0, "Rendering a Pie
Chart");
     };
}

// Context component that uses the strategy
@code {
    private IChartStrategy? chartStrategy;

    private void
SetChartStrategy(IChartStrategy strategy)
    {
        chartStrategy = strategy;
    }
}
```

In your Blazor component, you can now switch between different chart strategies dynamically:

```
<button @onclick="() => SetChartStrategy(new
LineChartStrategy())">Line Chart</button>
<button @onclick="() => SetChartStrategy(new
BarChartStrategy())">Bar Chart</button>
<button @onclick="() => SetChartStrategy(new
PieChartStrategy())">Pie Chart</button>

@if (chartStrategy != null)
{
    @chartStrategy.RenderChart()
}
```

This approach keeps the rendering logic for each chart type encapsulated, making the component easier to maintain and extend.

Factory Pattern

The Factory Pattern is a creational design pattern that provides an interface for creating objects in a superclass but allows subclasses to alter the type of objects that will be created. This pattern is particularly useful in Blazor when you need to create components or services dynamically based on runtime information.

Example in Blazor:

Suppose you have different types of notification components (e.g., success, error, warning) that need to be generated based on a specific condition.

```
// Define the product interface
public interface INotification
{
    RenderFragment Render();
}

// Concrete products
public class SuccessNotification :
INotification
{
    public RenderFragment Render() => builder
=>
    {
        builder.AddContent(0, "Success:
Operation completed successfully.");
    };
}

public class ErrorNotification : INotification
{
```

```csharp
    public RenderFragment Render() => builder
=>
    {
        builder.AddContent(0, "Error: Something
went wrong.");
    };
}

public class WarningNotification :
INotification
{
    public RenderFragment Render() => builder
=>
    {
        builder.AddContent(0, "Warning: Check
your inputs.");
    };
}

// The factory class
public class NotificationFactory
{
    public INotification
CreateNotification(string type) => type switch
    {
        "success" => new SuccessNotification(),
        "error" => new ErrorNotification(),
        "warning" => new WarningNotification(),
        _ => throw new
ArgumentException("Invalid notification type")
    };
}
```

In your Blazor component, you can use the factory to create the appropriate notification component:

```
@inject NotificationFactory notificationFactory

<button @onclick="(·) =>
ShowNotification('success')">Show
Success</button>
<button @onclick="() =>
ShowNotification('error')">Show Error</button>
```

```
<button @onclick="() =>
ShowNotification('warning')">Show
Warning</button>

@if (notification != null)
{
    @notification.Render()
}

@code {
    private INotification? notification;

    private void ShowNotification(string type)
    {
        notification =
notificationFactory.CreateNotification(type);
    }
}
```

Program.cs

```
builder.Services.AddScoped<NotificationFactory>
();
```

The Factory Pattern helps in centralizing the creation logic of various components, making the code more modular and easier to manage.

Composite Pattern

The Composite Pattern is a structural design pattern that allows you to compose objects into tree structures to represent part-whole hierarchies. It lets clients treat individual objects and compositions of objects uniformly. This pattern is particularly useful in UI frameworks like Blazor, where you may have components that contain collections of other components.

Example in Blazor:

Consider a scenario where you have a form component that contains various form elements (e.g., text fields, checkboxes, radio buttons). The Composite Pattern allows you to treat a group of form elements as a single component.

```
// Component interface
public interface IFormComponent
{
    RenderFragment Render();
}

// Leaf components
public class TextFieldComponent :
IFormComponent
{
    public RenderFragment Render() => builder
=>
    {
        builder.AddContent(0, "<input
type='text' />");
    };
}

public class CheckboxComponent : IFormComponent
{
    public RenderFragment Render() => builder
=>
    {
        builder.AddContent(0, "<input
type='checkbox' />");
    };
}

// Composite component
public class FormGroupComponent :
IFormComponent
{
```

```
    private readonly List<IFormComponent>
_children = new List<IFormComponent>();

    public void Add(IFormComponent component)
    {
        _children.Add(component);
    }

    public RenderFragment Render() => builder
=>
    {
        foreach (var child in _children)
        {
            builder.AddContent(0,
child.Render());
        }
    };
}
```

You can now build a composite form by combining individual form components:

```
@code {
    private FormGroupComponent formGroup = new
FormGroupComponent();

    protected override void OnInitialized()
    {
        formGroup.Add(new
TextFieldComponent());
        formGroup.Add(new CheckboxComponent());
        // Add more components as needed
    }
}

@formGroup.Render()
```

This example shows how the Composite Pattern can be used to manage complex UIs by treating individual components and their compositions in a uniform way.

Applying These Patterns within the Blazor Component Model

Applying these design patterns in Blazor enhances the flexibility, maintainability, and scalability of your component architecture.

- **Strategy Pattern** helps in dynamically switching behaviors (e.g., different rendering strategies) without cluttering your component logic with conditional statements.
- **Factory Pattern** centralizes the creation logic, making it easier to manage and extend the types of components your application can generate.
- **Composite Pattern** allows you to build complex UI structures from simpler components, facilitating the management of hierarchical component relationships.

By integrating these patterns into your Blazor projects, you can develop components that are both powerful and easy to manage, ensuring that your application architecture remains clean and adaptable as your project evolves.

Building a Component Library with Design Patterns

Creating a reusable component library in Blazor is a powerful way to promote code reuse, ensure consistency across projects, and streamline development workflows. By applying design patterns like Dependency Injection and the Observer Pattern, you can make your components more modular, maintainable, and scalable. This section will take an example-driven approach to illustrate how to build a component library that leverages these design patterns effectively.

Example-Driven Approach to Creating a Reusable Component Library

When building a component library, the goal is to create a set of reusable, generic components that can be easily integrated into different projects. These components should be well-documented, flexible, and designed to handle a variety of use cases.

Step 1: Define the Core Components

Start by defining the core components that will form the basis of your library. These might include common UI elements such as buttons, input fields, modals, and forms. Each component should be designed to be customizable through parameters, allowing developers to tailor them to specific needs without modifying the component's internal logic.

For example, consider a `ButtonComponent` that supports various styles and behaviors:

```razor
<!-- ButtonComponent.razor -->
<button class="@CssClass" @onclick="OnClick">
    @ChildContent
</button>

@code {
    [Parameter] public string CssClass { get;
set; } = "btn-default";
    [Parameter] public EventCallback OnClick
{ get; set; }
    [Parameter] public RenderFragment?
ChildContent { get; set; }
}
```

This button component is flexible enough to be used in different contexts, with customizable styling (CssClass) and behavior (OnClick). Developers can integrate this button into any project by simply passing in the appropriate parameters.

Step 2: Apply the Strategy and Factory Patterns

To make the library even more flexible, consider using the Strategy and Factory Patterns for components that need to handle different variations or behaviors.

Strategy Pattern Example:

Let's expand the button component to support different types of buttons, such as primary, secondary, or danger buttons, by applying the Strategy Pattern:

```
// Define the strategy interface
public interface IButtonStyleStrategy
{
    string GetCssClass();
}

// Implement concrete strategies
public class PrimaryButtonStrategy :
IButtonStyleStrategy
{
    public string GetCssClass() => "btn-
primary";
}

public class SecondaryButtonStrategy :
IButtonStyleStrategy
{
    public string GetCssClass() => "btn-
secondary";
}
```

```
public class DangerButtonStrategy :
IButtonStyleStrategy
{
    public string GetCssClass() => "btn-
danger";
}
```

Now, the `ButtonComponent` can dynamically switch styles based on the strategy:

```
<!-- ButtonComponent.razor -->
<button
class="@buttonStyleStrategy.GetCssClass()"
@onclick="OnClick">
    @ChildContent
</button>

@code {
    [Parameter] public IButtonStyleStrategy
buttonStyleStrategy { get; set; } = new
PrimaryButtonStrategy();
    [Parameter] public EventCallback OnClick
{ get; set; }
    [Parameter] public RenderFragment?
ChildContent { get; set; }
}
```

This setup allows developers to easily switch between button styles by passing the appropriate strategy to the component:

```
razor
<ButtonComponent buttonStyleStrategy="new
DangerButtonStrategy()" OnClick="HandleClick">
    Delete
</ButtonComponent>
```

Factory Pattern Example:

If your library needs to dynamically create different components at runtime, the Factory Pattern is ideal. For example, a `NotificationFactory` can be used to create different types of notifications:

```
// Define the product interface
public interface INotification
{
    RenderFragment Render();
}

// Concrete notification components
public class SuccessNotification :
INotification
{
    public RenderFragment Render() => builder
=>
    {
        builder.AddContent(0, "Success:
Operation completed successfully.");
    };
}

public class ErrorNotification : INotification
{
    public RenderFragment Render() => builder
=>
    {
        builder.AddContent(0, "Error: Something
went wrong.");
    };
}

// Factory class
public class NotificationFactory
{
    public INotification
CreateNotification(string type) => type switch
    {
        "success" => new SuccessNotification(),
        "error" => new ErrorNotification(),
        _ => throw new
ArgumentException("Invalid notification type")
    };
```

```
}
```

By using the factory, you can generate the appropriate
notification based on the runtime context:

```
@inject NotificationFactory notificationFactory

@if (notification != null)
{
    @notification.Render()
}

@code {
    private INotification? notification;

    private void ShowNotification(string type)
    {
        notification =
notificationFactory.CreateNotification(type);
    }
}
```

Integrating Patterns like Dependency Injection and Observer Pattern within Blazor Components

To further enhance your component library, you can
integrate more advanced patterns like Dependency
Injection (DI) and the Observer Pattern, which are crucial
for building scalable and decoupled systems.

Dependency Injection in Blazor Components

Dependency Injection is a core design pattern in Blazor
and .NET, allowing you to inject services and dependencies
directly into your components. This pattern promotes loose
coupling and enhances the testability and reusability of
your components.

Example:

Consider a `WeatherService` that fetches weather data from an API. By using DI, you can inject this service into any component that needs it:

```csharp
// WeatherService.cs
public class WeatherService
{
    private readonly HttpClient _httpClient;

    public WeatherService(HttpClient
httpClient)
    {
        _httpClient = httpClient;
    }

    public async Task<string>
GetWeatherAsync(string city)
    {
        var response = await
_httpClient.GetStringAsync($"weatherapi.com/{ci
ty}");
        return response;
    }
}

// Registration in Program.cs
builder.Services.AddScoped<WeatherService>();

// Usage in a Blazor component
@inject WeatherService weatherService

<p>@weatherData</p>

@code {
    private string weatherData = string.Empty;

    protected override async Task
OnInitializedAsync()
    {
```

```
        weatherData = await
weatherService.GetWeatherAsync("New York");
    }
}
```

By injecting `WeatherService`, you decouple the data-fetching logic from your component, making it easier to test and maintain.

Observer Pattern for Event Handling and State Management

The Observer Pattern is useful for managing event-driven communication between components, particularly in scenarios involving state changes or notifications. In Blazor, you can implement the Observer Pattern using events or by utilizing state management services.

Example:

Suppose you have a `NotificationService` that notifies components of new messages:

```
// NotificationService.cs
public class NotificationService
{
    public event Action<string>?
OnNotification;

    public void Notify(string message)
    {
        OnNotification?.Invoke(message);
    }
}

// Registration in Program.cs
builder.Services.AddSingleton<NotificationServi
ce>();
```

```
// Usage in a Blazor component
@inject NotificationService notificationService

<p>@notificationMessage</p>

@code {
    private string notificationMessage = "No
notifications";

    protected override void OnInitialized()
    {
        notificationService.OnNotification +=
HandleNotification;
    }

    private void HandleNotification(string
message)
    {
        notificationMessage = message;
        StateHasChanged();
    }

    public void Dispose()
    {
        notificationService.OnNotification -=
HandleNotification;
    }
}
```

In this example, the NotificationService acts as the subject, and any components subscribed to its notifications act as observers. This pattern is ideal for scenarios where multiple components need to react to the same event or state change.

Building a reusable component library with design patterns in Blazor allows you to create flexible, maintainable, and scalable UI components. By leveraging the Strategy, Factory, Dependency Injection, and Observer Patterns, you can ensure that your components are well-structured and adaptable to various use cases. Integrating these patterns into your Blazor component library not only improves code quality but also enhances the developer experience, making it easier to build and maintain large, complex applications.

Case Study: Implementing an Advanced UI Pattern

In this section, we'll walk through the process of building a complex UI component using design patterns in Blazor. We'll take a step-by-step approach to illustrate how these patterns can be applied to solve real-world challenges in UI development. By the end of this case study, you'll have a clear understanding of how to implement advanced design patterns in your own Blazor projects, along with insights into the challenges you might encounter and how to overcome them.

Step-by-Step Walkthrough of Building a Complex UI Component

Scenario: Building a Dynamic Dashboard Component

Imagine you're tasked with building a dynamic dashboard component for an enterprise application. The dashboard must be flexible, allowing users to configure and add different types of widgets (e.g., charts, lists, notifications) at runtime. The widgets need to be customizable, and the dashboard must support saving and loading configurations to and from a database.

To tackle this challenge, we'll apply several design patterns, including the Factory Pattern for widget creation, the Strategy Pattern for rendering different widget types, and the Observer Pattern for managing state and updates across the dashboard.

Step 1: Define the Widget Interface and Implement Concrete Widgets

First, define a common interface for all widgets to ensure that each widget type can be treated uniformly within the dashboard.

```
// IWidget.cs
public interface IWidget
{
    RenderFragment Render();
}

// Concrete widget implementations
public class ChartWidget : IWidget
{
    public RenderFragment Render() => builder
=>
    {
        builder.AddContent(0, "Rendering a
Chart Widget");
    };
}

public class ListWidget : IWidget
{
    public RenderFragment Render() => builder
=>
    {
        builder.AddContent(0, "Rendering a List
Widget");
    };
}

public class NotificationWidget : IWidget
{
    public RenderFragment Render() => builder
=>
    {
        builder.AddContent(0, "Rendering a
Notification Widget");
```

```
    };
}
```

Each widget implements the `IWidget` interface, encapsulating its specific rendering logic.

Step 2: Implement a Widget Factory

Next, create a factory class that dynamically generates widgets based on user input or configuration data.

```
// WidgetFactory.cs
public class WidgetFactory
{
    public IWidget CreateWidget(string
widgetType) => widgetType switch
    {
        "chart" => new ChartWidget(),
        "list" => new ListWidget(),
        "notification" => new
NotificationWidget(),
        _ => throw new
ArgumentException("Invalid widget type")
    };
}
```

This factory will be used by the dashboard component to create widgets as needed.

Step 3: Create the Dashboard Component

Now, build the main dashboard component that allows users to add and manage widgets. The dashboard will utilize the factory to instantiate widgets and the Strategy Pattern to render them appropriately.

```
@page "/dashboard"
@inject WidgetFactory widgetFactory
```

```
<div class="dashboard">
    <button @onclick="() =>
AddWidget('chart')">Add Chart</button>
    <button @onclick="() =>
AddWidget('list')">Add List</button>
    <button @onclick="() =>
AddWidget('notification')">Add
Notification</button>

    @foreach (var widget in widgets)
    {
        <div class="widget">
            @widget.Render()
            <button @onclick="() =>
RemoveWidget(widget)">Remove</button>
        </div>
    }
</div>

@code {
    private List<IWidget> widgets = new();

    private void AddWidget(string widgetType)
    {
        var widget =
widgetFactory.CreateWidget(widgetType);
        widgets.Add(widget);
    }

    private void RemoveWidget(IWidget widget)
    {
        widgets.Remove(widget);
    }
}
```

In this component:

- Users can add widgets by clicking the respective buttons.
- The `WidgetFactory` dynamically creates the appropriate widget based on the type.

74

- The dashboard maintains a list of widgets and renders them using their respective `Render` methods.

Step 4: Implement State Persistence Using the Observer Pattern

To enhance the dashboard, let's implement state persistence, allowing users to save and load their widget configurations. We'll use the Observer Pattern to manage state changes and notify the dashboard when the state needs to be updated.

```csharp
// DashboardState.cs
public class DashboardState
{
    private List<string> widgetTypes = new();
    public IReadOnlyList<string> WidgetTypes =>
widgetTypes.AsReadOnly();

    public event Action? OnChange;

    public void AddWidgetType(string
widgetType)
    {
        widgetTypes.Add(widgetType);
        NotifyStateChanged();
    }

    public void RemoveWidgetType(string
widgetType)
    {
        widgetTypes.Remove(widgetType);
        NotifyStateChanged();
    }

    private void NotifyStateChanged() =>
OnChange?.Invoke();
}
```

```
// Registration in Program.cs
builder.Services.AddSingleton<DashboardState>()
;

// Modifications to Dashboard.razor
@inject DashboardState dashboardState

@code {
    protected override void OnInitialized()
    {
        dashboardState.OnChange +=
UpdateWidgets;
    }

    private void AddWidget(string widgetType)
    {

dashboardState.AddWidgetType(widgetType);
        UpdateWidgets();
    }

    private void UpdateWidgets()
    {
        widgets.Clear();
        foreach (var widgetType in
dashboardState.WidgetTypes)
        {

widgets.Add(widgetFactory.CreateWidget(widgetTy
pe));
        }
        StateHasChanged();
    }

    public void Dispose()
    {
        dashboardState.OnChange -=
UpdateWidgets;
    }
}
```

In this implementation:

- The `DashboardState` service acts as the central store for widget types.
- The dashboard component subscribes to state changes and updates its list of widgets whenever the state changes.
- Users can add or remove widgets, and these changes are persisted in the `DashboardState`, allowing the dashboard to maintain its state across sessions.

Challenges Faced and Solutions Implemented

Building a complex UI component like the dynamic dashboard presents several challenges, especially when applying design patterns to ensure scalability and maintainability.

Challenge 1: Managing Dynamic Component Creation

- **Solution:** The Factory Pattern was key to managing the dynamic creation of widgets. By centralizing the creation logic, the dashboard can easily adapt to new widget types without requiring significant changes to the existing codebase.

Challenge 2: Synchronizing State Across Components

- **Solution:** The Observer Pattern allowed us to effectively manage and synchronize state across the dashboard and its widgets. By centralizing the state in the `DashboardState` service, we ensured that all components remain in sync, even as the state changes dynamically.

Challenge 3: Ensuring Scalability

- **Solution:** Applying the Strategy Pattern ensured that each widget type could be managed independently, making it easy to add new widget types in the future. This pattern also kept the dashboard's logic clean and focused on managing the overall structure, rather than the specifics of each widget.

Challenge 4: State Persistence

- **Solution:** Integrating state persistence using a singleton service (`DashboardState`) allowed the dashboard to maintain its configuration across sessions, enhancing the user experience and making the dashboard more robust.

This case study demonstrates how applying design patterns like the Factory Pattern, Strategy Pattern, and Observer Pattern can solve real-world challenges when building complex UI components in Blazor. By structuring the dashboard in a modular and scalable way, we've created a component that is not only flexible and reusable but also easy to maintain and extend. These patterns offer a powerful toolkit for tackling the complexities of modern UI development, ensuring that your Blazor applications are well-architected and future-proof.

Chapter 5: Enhancing Components with Advanced CSS and Styling Techniques

Styling is a crucial aspect of web development, and in Blazor, the ability to create visually appealing, responsive, and consistent UI components is vital for building modern web applications. In this chapter, we will explore advanced CSS and styling techniques that can be applied to Blazor components. You'll learn how to leverage CSS features such as variables, animations, and grid layouts to enhance your components, as well as how to use tools like CSS-in-JS and CSS frameworks for more dynamic styling. We'll also cover best practices for managing styles in large projects, ensuring that your Blazor applications are not only functional but also polished and professional. By the end of this chapter, you will have a solid understanding of how to effectively style your Blazor components to create a compelling user experience.

Integrating CSS into Blazor Components

Styling Blazor components effectively requires a balance between maintaining global consistency and enabling individual component customization. Blazor offers several approaches to integrating CSS, each with its own benefits depending on your project's needs. This section will cover CSS isolation, scoped styles, and global stylesheets, as well as how to leverage CSS variables and custom properties for theming and dynamic styling.

CSS Isolation, Scoped Styles, and Global Stylesheets

1. CSS Isolation:

CSS isolation is a feature in Blazor that allows you to create styles specific to a single component, ensuring that these styles do not affect other parts of your application. When you enable CSS isolation, Blazor automatically scopes the styles to the associated component, preventing unintended style leakage.

To use CSS isolation, you simply create a `.razor.css` file with the same name as your component. For example, if you have a component named `ButtonComponent.razor`, you would create a corresponding `ButtonComponent.razor.css` file:

```
/* ButtonComponent.razor.css */
button {
    background-color: #007bff;
    color: white;
    padding: 10px 20px;
    border-radius: 5px;
}
```

These styles are automatically scoped to the `ButtonComponent`, so they won't interfere with other buttons or elements in your application. The scoped styles are applied only to instances of the `ButtonComponent`, and Blazor ensures that the styles are unique to this component by appending a unique identifier to the CSS classes.

2. Scoped Styles Using `@key` and `@namespace`:

In addition to CSS isolation, you can manually scope styles within a component using the `@key` directive in Blazor.

This is particularly useful when you want to conditionally apply styles based on component state or properties.

```
<style>
    .my-component {
        background-color: lightblue;
    }
</style>

<div class="my-component" @key="componentId">
    <p>This is a scoped style example.</p>
</div>

@code {
    private string componentId =
Guid.NewGuid().ToString();
}
```

Here, the @key directive ensures that the style is applied uniquely to the specific instance of the component, which can be useful in scenarios where you have multiple instances of the same component with different states or content.

3. Global Stylesheets:

While CSS isolation is powerful, you may still need to define styles that apply globally across your entire application. For this, you can use global stylesheets that are included in your wwwroot directory and referenced in your App.razor file.

```
<!-- index.html -->
<link href="css/site.css" rel="stylesheet" />
```

Global styles are ideal for defining the overall theme of your application, such as typography, color schemes, and layout structures. These styles will apply to all components unless overridden by more specific styles in isolated or scoped stylesheets.

Leveraging CSS Variables and Custom Properties for Theming and Dynamic Styling

CSS variables, also known as custom properties, provide a powerful way to define and reuse values throughout your stylesheets. They are particularly useful for implementing theming and dynamic styling, as they allow you to change the appearance of your application based on user preferences or context without needing to modify the underlying CSS.

1. Defining CSS Variables:

CSS variables are defined using the -- syntax and can be scoped globally or within specific selectors. For instance, you might define a set of color variables in a global stylesheet:

```css
/* Global stylesheet (site.css) */
:root {
    --primary-color: #007bff;
    --secondary-color: #6c757d;
    --background-color: #f8f9fa;
}

body {
    background-color: var(--background-color);
    color: var(--secondary-color);
}
```

These variables can then be used throughout your stylesheets, making it easy to maintain consistency and implement theming.

2. Applying Themes Dynamically:

You can dynamically change the values of CSS variables to implement theming in your Blazor application. This can be done either through JavaScript interop or by modifying the styles directly within Blazor components.

```
<button @onclick="SetDarkTheme">Dark
Theme</button>
<button @onclick="SetLightTheme">Light
Theme</button>

@code {
    private void SetDarkTheme()
    {
        var root = document.documentElement;
        root.style.setProperty("--primary-
color", "#343a40");
        root.style.setProperty("--background-
color", "#212529");
        root.style.setProperty("--secondary-
color", "#adb5bd");
    }

    private void SetLightTheme()
    {
        var root = document.documentElement;
        root.style.setProperty("--primary-
color", "#007bff");
        root.style.setProperty("--background-
color", "#f8f9fa");
        root.style.setProperty("--secondary-
color", "#6c757d");
    }
}
```

This example demonstrates how to toggle between a dark and light theme by updating the CSS variables. This approach allows for dynamic theming without needing to reload or recompile the application.

3. Using CSS Variables in Isolated Styles:

CSS variables can also be used within isolated styles, allowing you to maintain consistency across different components while still benefiting from scoped styling.

```css
/* ButtonComponent.razor.css */
button {
    background-color: var(--primary-color);
    color: var(--secondary-color);
    padding: 10px 20px;
    border-radius: 5px;
}
```

Since the `ButtonComponent` uses global CSS variables, any changes to these variables will automatically reflect in the component's styling, ensuring consistency across your application.

Integrating CSS into Blazor components effectively requires a combination of CSS isolation, scoped styles, and global stylesheets. By leveraging these techniques, you can maintain a clean and organized styling strategy that minimizes conflicts and promotes reusability. Additionally, using CSS variables and custom properties allows for powerful theming and dynamic styling capabilities, making your Blazor applications more flexible and user-friendly. These tools and techniques are essential for building modern, visually appealing Blazor applications that can easily adapt to changing design requirements.

Advanced Layout Techniques

Creating responsive and visually consistent layouts is a key aspect of modern web development. In Blazor, advanced CSS layout techniques such as Flexbox and Grid can be utilized to build responsive and adaptive components that work well across different screen sizes and devices. Additionally, custom layout components can help manage complex UI scenarios by encapsulating layout logic in reusable components. This section explores how to use Flexbox and Grid for responsive Blazor components, and how to create custom layout components for more complex UI requirements.

Utilizing Flexbox and Grid for Responsive Blazor Components

1. Flexbox:

Flexbox is a powerful layout module in CSS that makes it easier to design flexible and responsive layouts. Flexbox layouts can adjust to different screen sizes and dynamically distribute space among items in a container, making it ideal for building responsive Blazor components.

Example: Responsive Navigation Bar:

```razor
<!-- NavBarComponent.razor -->
<nav class="navbar">
    <div class="navbar-brand">MyApp</div>
    <div class="navbar-links">
        <a href="/">Home</a>
        <a href="/about">About</a>
        <a href="/contact">Contact</a>
    </div>
</nav>

@code {
    // Component logic (if needed)
}

<style>
    .navbar {
        display: flex;
        justify-content: space-between;
```

```
        align-items: center;
        padding: 10px 20px;
        background-color: var(--primary-color);
        color: white;
    }

    .navbar-links a {
        margin-left: 20px;
        color: white;
        text-decoration: none;
    }

    .navbar-links a:hover {
        text-decoration: underline;
    }

    @media (max-width: 600px) {
        .navbar {
            flex-direction: column;
        }

        .navbar-links {
            display: flex;
            flex-direction: column;
            align-items: center;
        }

        .navbar-links a {
            margin: 10px 0;
        }
    }
</style>
```

In this example, the `NavBarComponent` uses Flexbox to align its elements. The `navbar` container is set to `display: flex`, which makes it a flex container with its children (`navbar-brand` and `navbar-links`) behaving as flex items. The `justify-content: space-between` rule ensures the brand and links are spaced apart, and the media query adjusts the layout for smaller screens by stacking the elements vertically.

2. CSS Grid:

CSS Grid is another powerful tool for creating complex, two-dimensional layouts. Unlike Flexbox, which is primarily designed for one-dimensional layouts (either rows or columns), Grid allows you to define both rows and columns, making it ideal for more complex layouts.

Example: Dashboard Layout:

```
<!-- DashboardComponent.razor -->
<div class="dashboard">
    <div class="header">Header</div>
    <div class="sidebar">Sidebar</div>
    <div class="content">Main Content</div>
    <div class="footer">Footer</div>
</div>

@code {
    // Component logic (if needed)
}

<style>
    .dashboard {
        display: grid;
        grid-template-areas:
            "header header"
            "sidebar content"
            "footer footer";
        grid-template-columns: 200px 1fr;
        grid-template-rows: auto 1fr auto;
        height: 100vh;
    }

    .header {
        grid-area: header;
        background-color: var(--primary-color);
        color: white;
        padding: 10px;
    }

    .sidebar {
```

```
        grid-area: sidebar;
        background-color: var(--secondary-
color);
        color: white;
        padding: 10px;
    }

    .content {
        grid-area: content;
        padding: 20px;
    }

    .footer {
        grid-area: footer;
        background-color: var(--primary-color);
        color: white;
        padding: 10px;
    }

    @media (max-width: 600px) {
        .dashboard {
            grid-template-areas:
                "header"
                "content"
                "sidebar"
                "footer";
            grid-template-columns: 1fr;
            grid-template-rows: auto 1fr auto
auto;
        }
    }
</style>
```

In this example, the `DashboardComponent` uses CSS Grid to create a structured layout with defined areas for the header, sidebar, content, and footer. The `grid-template-areas` property specifies the layout regions, while `grid-template-columns` and `grid-template-rows` define the sizes of the columns and rows. The media query adjusts the layout for smaller screens by stacking all areas vertically.

Creating Custom Layout Components for Complex UI Scenarios

For more complex UI scenarios, it's often beneficial to encapsulate layout logic within custom Blazor layout components. This allows you to reuse complex layouts across your application and keep your Razor pages and components clean and maintainable.

1. Custom Layout Components:

Blazor supports the concept of layout components, which can be used to define a consistent structure for your pages or components. You can create a custom layout component to encapsulate a complex layout and apply it to multiple pages or components.

Example: Creating a Custom Layout Component:

```
<!-- CustomLayout.razor -->
@inherits LayoutComponentBase

<div class="custom-layout">
    <header>
        @Body
    </header>
    <div class="layout-content">
        @ChildContent
    </div>
    <footer>
        © 2024 MyCompany
    </footer>
</div>

<style>
    .custom-layout {
        display: flex;
        flex-direction: column;
        height: 100vh;
```

```css
    }

    header {
        background-color: var(--primary-color);
        padding: 20px;
        color: white;
        text-align: center;
    }

    .layout-content {
        flex: 1;
        padding: 20px;
    }

    footer {
        background-color: var(--secondary-
color);
        padding: 10px;
        color: white;
        text-align: center;
    }
</style>
```

In this `CustomLayout` component:

- `@Body` represents the main content area, which is typically used for the page's content.
- `@ChildContent` allows you to insert additional content within the layout.
- The layout is styled using Flexbox to ensure it stretches to fill the viewport, with a fixed header and footer and a flexible content area in between.

2. Applying the Custom Layout to Pages:

Once your custom layout component is created, you can apply it to any page by specifying it with the `@layout` directive.

```
@page "/example"
```

```
@layout CustomLayout

<h1>Example Page</h1>
<p>This is an example page using the custom
layout.</p>
```

This approach ensures that all pages using the CustomLayout share a consistent structure and styling, which is particularly useful in large applications with many pages that need to adhere to a uniform design.

Advanced layout techniques, such as using Flexbox and Grid, provide powerful tools for creating responsive and complex layouts in Blazor applications. By mastering these techniques, you can design components that adapt seamlessly to different screen sizes and user contexts. Additionally, creating custom layout components allows you to encapsulate and reuse complex layout logic, promoting consistency and maintainability across your application. These strategies are essential for developing modern, user-friendly Blazor applications that deliver a polished and professional experience.

Animation and Transitions

Animations and transitions are essential tools for enhancing the user experience in web applications. They can make interactions feel more fluid, guide the user's attention, and add a level of polish that makes an application feel more professional and engaging. In Blazor, you can integrate CSS animations and transitions to create visually appealing effects, and even trigger these animations programmatically from your components. This section explores how to use CSS animations and transitions within Blazor components, as well as how to control them dynamically through Blazor's powerful event and state management capabilities.

Integrating CSS Animations and Transitions for Enhancing User Experience

1. CSS Transitions:

CSS transitions allow you to smoothly animate the change of properties over a specified duration. They are ideal for animating changes in size, position, color, opacity, and other CSS properties when an element's state changes, such as on hover or when a class is toggled.

Example: Hover Effect on a Button:

```razor
<!-- AnimatedButtonComponent.razor -->
<button class="animated-button">
    Hover over me
</button>

<style>
    .animated-button {
        background-color: #007bff;
        color: white;
        padding: 10px 20px;
        border: none;
        border-radius: 5px;
        transition: background-color 0.3s ease,
transform 0.3s ease;
    }

    .animated-button:hover {
        background-color: #0056b3;
        transform: scale(1.1);
    }
</style>
```

In this example, the `animated-button` class uses the `transition` property to animate the background color and scale of the button when the user hovers over it. The transition is smooth and lasts for 0.3 seconds, creating a more engaging and responsive user experience.

2. CSS Animations:

CSS animations are more powerful than transitions, allowing you to define keyframes for more complex animations. You can control the animation's timing, duration, and even loop it indefinitely or a set number of times.

Example: Keyframe Animation on a Loading Spinner:

```
<!-- LoadingSpinnerComponent.razor -->
<div class="spinner"></div>

<style>
    .spinner {
        width: 50px;
        height: 50px;
        border: 5px solid #f3f3f3;
        border-top: 5px solid #007bff;
        border-radius: 50%;
        animation: spin 1s linear infinite;
    }

    @keyframes spin {
        0% { transform: rotate(0deg); }
        100% { transform: rotate(360deg); }
    }
</style>
```

This `spinner` element is animated using the `spin` keyframes, which rotate the element 360 degrees over one second. The animation is set to loop infinitely, creating a continuous spinning effect, perfect for indicating loading states.

Triggering Animations Programmatically from Blazor Components

In addition to using CSS for animations, you might want to trigger animations programmatically from within your Blazor components. This can be useful when you need to animate elements in response to user interactions, state changes, or other events that occur in your application.

1. Triggering CSS Animations with Conditional Classes:

One simple way to trigger animations programmatically is by conditionally applying CSS classes based on component state. Blazor's binding and event system make it easy to toggle classes dynamically.

Example: Fade In/Out Animation on a Modal:

```razor
<!-- ModalComponent.razor -->
<div class="modal-overlay @modalClass"
@onclick="CloseModal">
    <div class="modal-content"
@onclick:stopPropagation="true">
        <h2>Modal Title</h2>
        <p>Modal content goes here...</p>
        <button
@onclick="CloseModal">Close</button>
    </div>
</div>

@code {
    private string modalClass = "hidden";

    public void ShowModal()
    {
        modalClass = "fade-in";
    }
```

```
    private void CloseModal()
    {
        modalClass = "fade-out";
    }
}

<style>
    .modal-overlay {
        display: none;
        position: fixed;
        top: 0;
        left: 0;
        width: 100%;
        height: 100%;
        background: rgba(0, 0, 0, 0.5);
        justify-content: center;
        align-items: center;
        transition: opacity 0.5s ease;
    }

    .modal-content {
        background: white;
        padding: 20px;
        border-radius: 5px;
    }

    .fade-in {
        display: flex;
        opacity: 0;
        animation: fadeIn 0.5s forwards;
    }

    .fade-out {
        animation: fadeOut 0.5s forwards;
    }

    .hidden {
        display: none;
    }

    @keyframes fadeIn {
        to { opacity: 1; }
    }
```

```
@keyframes fadeOut {
    to { opacity: 0; }
}
</style>
```

In this example, the `modalClass` is toggled between `fade-in` and `fade-out` when showing or closing the modal. The `fade-in` animation makes the modal appear smoothly, while the `fade-out` animation hides it in a similarly smooth fashion. The modal also has a `hidden` class to ensure it's not rendered at all when not in use.

2. Triggering Animations Using JavaScript Interop:

For more advanced scenarios, such as triggering animations that aren't easily managed with CSS alone, you can use Blazor's JavaScript Interop to invoke JavaScript functions that control animations.

Example: Triggering a Custom Animation Using JavaScript:

```
<!-- AnimatedBoxComponent.razor -->
<div id="animated-box"
@onclick="TriggerAnimation">Click me to
animate</div>

@code {
    [Inject] private IJSRuntime JS { get;
set; } = default!;

    private async Task TriggerAnimation()
    {
        await JS.InvokeVoidAsync("animateBox");
    }
}

<style>
    #animated-box {
        width: 100px;
```

```
        height: 100px;
        background-color: #007bff;
        margin: 20px;
        cursor: pointer;
    }
</style>
```

JavaScript Code (in `wwwroot/js/site.js`):

```
function animateBox() {
    const box =
document.getElementById('animated-box');
    box.style.transition = 'transform 0.5s';
    box.style.transform = 'translateX(100px)';
}
```

Here, the `TriggerAnimation` method uses JavaScript Interop to call the `animateBox` function in the browser's JavaScript context. This function applies a transform to the `#animated-box` element, making it move horizontally when clicked.

Integrating CSS animations and transitions into your Blazor components can significantly enhance the user experience by adding visual feedback and smooth transitions. Whether you're using simple CSS transitions or more complex animations with keyframes, these effects make your application feel more dynamic and responsive. Additionally, by triggering animations programmatically using conditional classes or JavaScript Interop, you can create interactive and context-sensitive animations that respond to user actions or state changes. Mastering these techniques will allow you to build visually compelling Blazor applications that delight users with smooth, polished interactions.

Chapter 6: Handling Accessibility and Internationalization

Building applications that are accessible and available to users across different languages and regions is more important than ever. Accessibility ensures that your Blazor applications are usable by people of all abilities, including those with disabilities. Meanwhile, internationalization allows your application to reach a broader audience by supporting multiple languages and cultural contexts. In this chapter, we will explore strategies and best practices for incorporating accessibility and internationalization into your Blazor components. By mastering these concepts, you'll be able to create applications that are not only compliant with accessibility standards but also adaptable to the diverse needs of users around the world.

Building Accessible Components

Building accessible UI components in Blazor is essential to ensure that your application can be used by everyone, including people with disabilities. Accessibility isn't just a legal requirement in many regions; it's also a key factor in providing a positive user experience for all. This section will cover best practices for creating accessible components in Blazor, including how to use ARIA (Accessible Rich Internet Applications) attributes effectively and how to ensure that your components are fully keyboard-navigable.

Configuration

1. Install the Required NuGet Packages
Ensure that your project has the necessary packages installed. You need to add the following package:

dotnet add package Microsoft.Extensions.Localization

2. Set Up Localization in Your Project

You need to configure the Blazor application to support localization.

Configure Services in Program.cs (or Startup.cs in older templates):

Add the localization services and configure them:

```
using Microsoft.Extensions.DependencyInjection;
using System.Globalization;

var builder =
WebApplication.CreateBuilder(args);

// Add services to the container.
builder.Services.AddRazorPages();
builder.Services.AddServerSideBlazor();

// Add localization services
builder.Services.AddLocalization(options =>
options.ResourcesPath = "Resources");

var app = builder.Build();

// Configure the localization middleware
var supportedCultures = new[] { "en-US", "fr-
FR" };
var localizationOptions = new
RequestLocalizationOptions()
    .SetDefaultCulture(supportedCultures[0])
    .AddSupportedCultures(supportedCultures)
    .AddSupportedUICultures(supportedCultures);

app.UseRequestLocalization(localizationOptions)
;

// Configure the HTTP request pipeline.
```

```
app.UseStaticFiles();
app.UseRouting();

app.MapBlazorHub();
app.MapFallbackToPage("/_Host");

app.Run();
```

This example supports English (en-US) and French (fr-FR). Modify the cultures as per your needs.

Best Practices for Creating Accessible UI Components in Blazor

1. Use Semantic HTML:

Using semantic HTML elements is one of the simplest and most effective ways to enhance accessibility. Semantic elements, like `<nav>`, `<header>`, `<main>`, `<footer>`, `<button>`, `<form>`, and others, provide meaningful information to assistive technologies such as screen readers. This helps users who rely on these technologies to better understand and navigate your application.

```
<!-- Example of Semantic HTML -->
<nav>
    <ul>
        <li><a href="/home">Home</a></li>
        <li><a href="/about">About</a></li>
        <li><a href="/contact">Contact</a></li>
    </ul>
</nav>

<main>
    <h1>Welcome to Our Website</h1>
    <p>This is the main content area.</p>
</main>
```

By using semantic elements, you make it easier for assistive technologies to interpret your content and convey it correctly to users.

2. Provide Alternative Text for Images:

All images should include an `alt` attribute that describes the content or function of the image. This text is read by screen readers, ensuring that visually impaired users can understand the purpose of the image.

```razor
<img src="logo.png" alt="Company Logo" />
```

If the image is purely decorative and doesn't add meaningful content, you can set the `alt` attribute to an empty string (`alt=""`), which will instruct screen readers to ignore the image.

3. Ensure Sufficient Color Contrast:

Ensure that the text and background colors used in your components have sufficient contrast. This is crucial for users with visual impairments, such as color blindness or low vision. Tools like the WebAIM Contrast Checker can help you verify that your color choices meet accessibility guidelines (WCAG 2.1).

```css
/* Example of sufficient contrast */
.button {
    background-color: #007bff;
    color: white;
    padding: 10px 20px;
    border: none;
    border-radius: 5px;
}
```

Techniques for ARIA Integration and Ensuring Keyboard Navigability

1. ARIA Integration:

ARIA (Accessible Rich Internet Applications) attributes help bridge the gap when native HTML elements and semantics are not enough to convey the role, state, or properties of UI components. By integrating ARIA attributes into your Blazor components, you can provide additional context to assistive technologies.

- **Role:** Define the role of a non-semantic element to help assistive technologies understand its purpose.

```
<div role="alert">This is an important message.</div>
```

- **State:** Use ARIA attributes to describe the current state of an element, especially for interactive components.

```
<button aria-expanded="@isExpanded" @onclick="ToggleDropdown">Toggle Dropdown</button>
<ul class="@dropdownClass" aria-hidden="@(isExpanded ? "false" : "true")">
    <li><a href="#">Item 1</a></li>
    <li><a href="#">Item 2</a></li>
</ul>

@code {
    private bool isExpanded = false;
    private string dropdownClass =>
isExpanded ? "dropdown show" : "dropdown hide";

    private void ToggleDropdown() => isExpanded
= !isExpanded;
}
```

In this example, the `aria-expanded` attribute informs screen readers whether the dropdown is currently expanded, while `aria-hidden` indicates whether the dropdown content is visible.

2. Ensuring Keyboard Navigability:

Keyboard navigability is critical for users who rely on keyboards instead of a mouse. To ensure that your Blazor components are keyboard accessible, consider the following practices:

- **Use the `tabindex` Attribute:** The `tabindex` attribute allows you to control the order in which elements receive focus when the user presses the Tab key. This is especially useful for custom components or when the default tab order is not logical.

```
<div tabindex="0">Focusable Div</div>
```

- **Provide Focus Indicators:** Ensure that interactive elements, such as links and buttons, have a visible focus state, making it clear to users which element is currently active.

```
.button:focus {
    outline: 2px solid #0056b3;
    outline-offset: 2px;
}
```

- **Trap Focus in Modal Dialogs:** When displaying a modal dialog, it's important to trap focus within the modal so that keyboard users cannot tab outside of it until the dialog is closed.

```
@code {
```

```
    private ElementReference modalRef;

    private async Task TrapFocus()
    {
        await JS.InvokeVoidAsync("trapFocus",
modalRef);
    }
}
```

JavaScript Code (in `wwwroot/js/site.js`):

```javascript
function trapFocus(element) {
    const focusableEls =
element.querySelectorAll('a, button, input,
[tabindex]:not([tabindex="-1"])');
    const firstFocusableEl = focusableEls[0];
    const lastFocusableEl =
focusableEls[focusableEls.length - 1];

    element.addEventListener('keydown',
function(e) {
        const isTabPressed = (e.key === 'Tab'
|| e.keyCode === 9);

        if (!isTabPressed) return;

        if (e.shiftKey) {
            if (document.activeElement ===
firstFocusableEl) {
                lastFocusableEl.focus();
                e.preventDefault();
            }
        } else {
            if (document.activeElement ===
lastFocusableEl) {
                firstFocusableEl.focus();
                e.preventDefault();
            }
        }
    });
}
```

This JavaScript function traps the focus within a modal dialog, preventing the user from tabbing out of the modal until they close it.

Building accessible Blazor components requires thoughtful application of semantic HTML, ARIA attributes, and keyboard accessibility practices. By following best practices and integrating accessibility features directly into your components, you ensure that your application is usable by a wider audience, including those with disabilities. These practices not only improve the overall user experience but also help you comply with accessibility standards, making your application more inclusive and welcoming to all users.

Internationalization (i18n) and Localization (l10n)

As applications become more global, the need to support multiple languages and cultural contexts becomes critical. Internationalization (i18n) and localization (l10n) are processes that allow your Blazor components to adapt to different languages and cultural conventions. This ensures that your application can reach and serve a diverse audience, regardless of their language or region. This section will cover strategies for making components multilingual and handling date, time, and number formatting in different cultures.

Strategies for Making Components Multilingual

Internationalizing your Blazor application involves designing your components to support multiple languages, while localization involves providing the specific translations and cultural settings required for each language or region.

1. Using `.resx` Files for Localization:

One common strategy in .NET for localization is to use resource files (`.resx`). These files store key-value pairs where the key is a unique identifier, and the value is the localized text. Each language or culture has its own `.resx` file.

Example: Setting Up Resource Files

- Create a `Resources` folder in your Blazor project.
- Add a default resource file, such as `Strings.resx`, for the base language (usually English).
- Add additional resource files for other languages, such as `Strings.fr.resx` for French or `Strings.es.resx` for Spanish.

Strings.resx (default)

Name	Value
Greeting	Hello, World!

Strings.fr.resx (French)

Name	Value
Greeting	Bonjour, le monde!

Example: Accessing Localized Strings in Blazor

```
@inject IStringLocalizer<Resources.Strings>
Localizer

<h1>@Localizer["Greeting"]</h1>
```

106

In this example, the `IStringLocalizer` service is injected into the Blazor component to retrieve the localized string based on the current culture. If the application's culture is set to French, it will display "Bonjour, le monde!" instead of "Hello, World!".

2. Switching Languages Dynamically:

To make your application more dynamic, you can allow users to switch languages at runtime. This involves updating the application's culture and refreshing the UI.

Example: Language Switcher

```
@inject IStringLocalizer<Resources.Strings>
Localizer
@inject NavigationManager Navigation

<select @onchange="ChangeLanguage">
    <option value="en">English</option>
    <option value="fr">Français</option>
</select>

<h1>@Localizer["Greeting"]</h1>

@code {
    private async Task
ChangeLanguage(ChangeEventArgs e)
    {
        var selectedLanguage =
e.Value.ToString();
        CultureInfo newCulture = new
CultureInfo(selectedLanguage);

        // Set the culture
        CultureInfo.DefaultThreadCurrentCulture
= newCulture;

CultureInfo.DefaultThreadCurrentUICulture =
newCulture;
```

```
            // Reload the page to apply the changes
            Navigation.NavigateTo(Navigation.Uri,
forceLoad: true);
    }
}
```

In this example, a dropdown menu allows users to select their preferred language. When the language is changed, the application updates the current culture and reloads the page to reflect the changes.

3. Localizing Component Parameters:

If your components accept text or other user-visible strings as parameters, ensure these parameters are also localized.

Example: Localized Button Component

```
<!-- LocalizedButton.razor -->
<button>@Label</button>

@code {
    [Parameter] public string Label { get;
set; } = "Click me";
}
```

Usage:

```
<LocalizedButton
Label="@Localizer["SubmitButton"]" />
```

This approach allows you to pass localized strings to components, ensuring that all user-facing text is consistent with the selected language.

Handling Date, Time, and Number Formatting in Different Cultures

Different cultures have different conventions for formatting dates, times, numbers, and currencies. To provide a seamless experience for users across different regions, it's important to format these elements according to the user's locale.

1. Date and Time Formatting:

In .NET, you can format dates and times using the `DateTime.ToString()` method with culture-specific format strings.

Example: Displaying a Localized Date

```
@code {
    private DateTime today = DateTime.Now;
}

<p>@today.ToString("D",
CultureInfo.CurrentCulture)</p>
```

In this example, the date will be displayed according to the current culture's long date pattern. For instance, in the US, it might display as "Monday, August 15, 2024", while in France, it would be "lundi 15 août 2024".

2. Number and Currency Formatting:

Number formatting varies widely between cultures, particularly with respect to decimal separators, thousand separators, and currency symbols.

Example: Localized Number and Currency Formatting

```
@code {
    private decimal price = 1234.56m;
}
```

```
<p>@price.ToString("C",
CultureInfo.CurrentCulture)</p>
```

The "C" format specifier formats the number as a currency value. In the US, the output would be "$1,234.56", while in Germany, it would be "1.234,56 €".

3. Handling Time Zones:

When working with time-sensitive data, it's important to consider the user's local time zone. Blazor provides mechanisms to handle time zones appropriately.

Example: Converting UTC to Local Time

```
@code {
    private DateTime utcTime = DateTime.UtcNow;

    private DateTime LocalTime =>
utcTime.ToLocalTime();
}

<p>UTC Time: @utcTime.ToString("f",
CultureInfo.CurrentCulture)</p>
<p>Local Time: @LocalTime.ToString("f",
CultureInfo.CurrentCulture)</p>
```

This example converts a UTC time to the user's local time using `ToLocalTime()`, ensuring that time displays are accurate for the user's region.

Internationalization and localization are critical for making your Blazor components accessible to a global audience. By implementing multilingual support using resource files, enabling dynamic language switching, and formatting dates, times, and numbers according to cultural norms, you can create a more inclusive and user-friendly application. Handling these aspects properly ensures that users across different languages and regions have a consistent and pleasant experience with your application, no matter where they are located.

Case Study: Designing a Globally Accessible Component

In this case study, we will walk through the process of designing a Blazor component that fully supports both accessibility and internationalization. This end-to-end example will demonstrate how to build a component that can be used by people with disabilities and is adaptable to different languages and cultures. By the end of this case study, you will understand how to combine accessibility best practices with internationalization techniques to create a truly global component.

Scenario: Building an Accessible and Localized Date Picker Component

Let's say you need to create a date picker component that allows users to select a date from a calendar. This component must be:

- **Accessible:** Fully usable with a keyboard and screen readers, and compliant with ARIA standards.
- **Localized:** Able to display the date in different languages and formats based on the user's locale, and provide translated labels and messages.

Step 1: Define the Component Structure with Semantic HTML

Start by defining the structure of the date picker using semantic HTML elements. This ensures that assistive

technologies can understand the component's role and
structure.

```razor
<!-- DatePicker.razor -->
<div class="date-picker">
    <label for="date-input">@Localizer["SelectDate"]</label>
    <input id="date-input" type="text"
@bind="selectedDateString"
@onfocus="ToggleCalendar"
@onkeydown="HandleKeyDown" aria-
expanded="@calendarVisible" aria-
controls="calendar" aria-describedby="calendar-
instructions" />

    <div id="calendar" class="calendar"
@key="calendarVisible"
style="display:@(calendarVisible ? "block" :
"none")" aria-hidden="@(!calendarVisible)">
        <p id="calendar-instructions"
class="sr-
only">@Localizer["CalendarInstructions"]</p>
        @foreach (var week in calendarWeeks)
        {
            <div class="calendar-row">
                @foreach (var day in week)
                {
                    <button class="calendar-day
@GetDayClass(day)" @onclick="() =>
SelectDate(day)" tabindex="-1" aria-
selected="@(day == selectedDate)">
                        @day.Day
                    </button>
                }
            </div>
        }
    </div>
</div>

@code {
    [Inject] private
IStringLocalizer<Resources.Strings> Localizer
{ get; set; } = default!;
```

112

```
    private bool calendarVisible = false;
    private string selectedDateString = "";
    private DateTime selectedDate =
DateTime.Today;
    private List<List<DateTime>> calendarWeeks
= new();

    protected override void OnInitialized()
    {
        GenerateCalendar();
        selectedDateString =
selectedDate.ToString("d",
CultureInfo.CurrentCulture);
    }

    private void ToggleCalendar()
    {
        calendarVisible = !calendarVisible;
    }

    private void SelectDate(DateTime date)
    {
        selectedDate = date;
        selectedDateString = date.ToString("d",
CultureInfo.CurrentCulture);
        calendarVisible = false;
    }

    private void
HandleKeyDown(KeyboardEventArgs e)
    {
        if (e.Key == "Enter" || e.Key == " " ||
e.Key == "ArrowDown")
        {
            ToggleCalendar();
        }
    }

    private void GenerateCalendar()
    {
        var firstDayOfMonth = new
DateTime(selectedDate.Year, selectedDate.Month,
1);
```

```csharp
        var lastDayOfMonth =
firstDayOfMonth.AddMonths(1).AddDays(-1);
        var firstDayOfCalendar =
firstDayOfMonth.AddDays(-
(int)firstDayOfMonth.DayOfWeek);
        var lastDayOfCalendar =
lastDayOfMonth.AddDays(6 -
(int)lastDayOfMonth.DayOfWeek);

        var day = firstDayOfCalendar;
        while (day <= lastDayOfCalendar)
        {
            var week = new List<DateTime>();
            for (int i = 0; i < 7; i++)
            {
                week.Add(day);
                day = day.AddDays(1);
            }
            calendarWeeks.Add(week);
        }
    }

    private string GetDayClass(DateTime day)
    {
        return day == selectedDate ?
"selected" : day.Month != selectedDate.Month ?
"out-of-month" : "";
    }
}
```

Step 2: Integrate ARIA for Accessibility

To ensure the date picker is accessible, we use ARIA
attributes to describe the component's functionality and
state to assistive technologies.

- **aria-expanded and aria-controls:** These
  attributes on the input element indicate whether the
  calendar is expanded and which element it controls.
- **aria-hidden:** This attribute on the calendar hides it
  from screen readers when it's not visible.

- **aria-selected:** This attribute on each day button marks the currently selected date.
- **aria-describedby:** This attribute on the input links to an off-screen instruction label, providing additional guidance to screen reader users.

Adding ARIA Instructions:

```
<p id="calendar-instructions" class="sr-
only">@Localizer["CalendarInstructions"]</p>
```

The `sr-only` class is used to visually hide the instructions while keeping them accessible to screen readers.

Step 3: Localize Labels, Messages, and Date Formats

To make the component multilingual, we use the `IStringLocalizer` service to fetch localized strings. The date format is adjusted according to the user's current culture using the `ToString` method with culture-specific formatting.

Resource Strings:

Strings.resx (default)

Name	Value
SelectDate	Select a Date
CalendarInstructions	Use the arrow keys to navigate dates.

Strings.fr.resx (French)

Name	Value
SelectDate	Sélectionner une date
CalendarInstructions	Utilisez les touches fléchées pour naviguer entre les dates.

Localized Date Display:

```
@code {
    selectedDateString =
selectedDate.ToString("d",
CultureInfo.CurrentCulture);
}
```

This ensures that the date is displayed in the format appropriate to the user's locale. For example, "12/31/2024" in the US might be displayed as "31/12/2024" in France.

Step 4: Ensure Keyboard Navigability

The date picker component must be fully operable using only the keyboard. Key functionality includes:

- **Opening the calendar:** The calendar opens when the user focuses on the input and presses Enter, Space, or Arrow Down.
- **Navigating the calendar:** Once open, the user can navigate the dates using the arrow keys (enhancements like this can be added later).
- **Selecting a date:** The date is selected when the user presses Enter or clicks a date.

Handling Key Events:

```
@code {
    private void
HandleKeyDown(KeyboardEventArgs e)
    {
```

```
        if (e.Key == "Enter" || e.Key == " " ||
e.Key == "ArrowDown")
        {
            ToggleCalendar();
        }
    }
}
```

This case study illustrates how to build a globally accessible and localized date picker component in Blazor. By integrating ARIA attributes, ensuring keyboard navigability, and supporting multiple languages and cultures, you create a component that is not only inclusive but also adaptable to users around the world. This approach ensures that your application meets accessibility standards while providing a seamless experience for users in different regions, enhancing the overall usability and reach of your Blazor applications.

Chapter 7: Testing and Debugging Advanced Blazor Components

As Blazor applications grow in complexity, ensuring their reliability and performance becomes increasingly important. Testing and debugging advanced Blazor components are crucial steps in the development process, helping you identify and fix issues before they impact users. This chapter focuses on the strategies and tools available for testing and debugging Blazor components. You'll learn how to write unit tests, use test frameworks effectively, and debug complex components to ensure that your application is robust and maintainable. By mastering these techniques, you can build high-quality Blazor applications that are both stable and efficient, providing a seamless experience for your users.

Unit Testing Blazor Components

Unit testing is an essential practice in software development, helping ensure that individual components work as expected and continue to function correctly as your code evolves. For Blazor applications, unit testing involves verifying that components render correctly, handle user interactions appropriately, and manage state effectively. This section will cover the tools and frameworks available for unit testing Blazor components, with a focus on bUnit, a popular testing library. We'll also explore best practices for writing and organizing unit tests for complex Blazor components.

Tools and Frameworks for Unit Testing

1. bUnit:

bUnit is a powerful testing library specifically designed for Blazor components. It allows you to write unit tests for your components using familiar testing frameworks like xUnit, NUnit, or MSTest. With bUnit, you can render components, interact with them, and verify their output in a simple and intuitive way.

Key Features of bUnit:

- **Component rendering:** Render Blazor components in a test context.
- **Event simulation:** Simulate user interactions, such as clicks or form submissions.
- **Markup verification:** Compare the rendered markup against expected HTML.
- **Dependency injection:** Inject services and dependencies into components under test.

Example: Setting Up bUnit with xUnit

First, add the necessary NuGet packages to your test project:

```
dotnet add package bunit
dotnet add package xunit
```

Next, create a basic test setup in your test project:

```
using Bunit;
using Xunit;
using MyBlazorApp.Components; // Replace with
your component's namespace

public class MyComponentTests : TestContext
{
    [Fact]
```

```
    public void
MyComponent_Should_RenderCorrectly()
    {
        // Arrange
        var cut =
RenderComponent<MyComponent>();

        // Act & Assert
        cut.MarkupMatches("<h1>Hello,
World!</h1>");
    }
}
```

In this example, the `RenderComponent<MyComponent>()` method renders the `MyComponent` component in a test context, and `MarkupMatches()` checks if the rendered output matches the expected HTML.

Writing and Organizing Unit Tests for Complex Components

When dealing with complex components, it's important to structure your tests in a way that ensures clarity and maintainability. Here's how you can approach writing and organizing unit tests for more advanced scenarios:

1. Test Structure and Naming Conventions:

Organize your tests into categories based on the functionality they are testing, such as rendering, interactions, and state management. Use descriptive test names that clearly convey what the test is verifying.

```
public class DatePickerTests : TestContext
{
    [Fact]
```

```csharp
    public void
DatePicker_Should_RenderDefaultDate_When_Loaded
()
    {
        var cut =
RenderComponent<DatePicker>();

        cut.MarkupMatches("<input type=\"text\"
value=\"12/31/2024\" />");
    }

    [Fact]
    public void
DatePicker_Should_ToggleCalendarVisibility_When
_InputIsClicked()
    {
        var cut =
RenderComponent<DatePicker>();

        cut.Find("input").Click();

        Assert.Contains("calendar",
cut.Markup);
    }

    [Fact]
    public void
DatePicker_Should_SelectDate_When_DayIsClicked(
)
    {
        var cut =
RenderComponent<DatePicker>();
        cut.Find("input").Click();

        cut.Find(".calendar-day").Click();

        Assert.Equal("01/01/2025",
cut.Instance.SelectedDateString);
    }
}
```

2. Testing Interactions:

Complex components often involve user interactions, such as clicking buttons, typing in text fields, or selecting options. bUnit allows you to simulate these interactions and verify the resulting component state.

Example: Simulating User Interaction

```
[Fact]
public void
Modal_Should_OpenAndClose_When_ToggleButtonIsCl
icked()
{
    var cut =
RenderComponent<ModalComponent>();

    var button = cut.Find("button");
    button.Click();

    Assert.True(cut.Instance.IsOpen); // Verify
that the modal is open

    button.Click();

    Assert.False(cut.Instance.IsOpen); //
Verify that the modal is closed
}
```

In this example, we simulate clicks on a button that toggles the visibility of a modal and verify that the component's state (IsOpen) updates correctly.

3. Testing State Management:

State management is a critical aspect of complex components, particularly those that involve dynamic data or user input. Tests should verify that state changes are handled correctly and that the component behaves as expected in different states.

Example: Testing State Changes

```
[Fact]
public void
Counter_Should_IncrementValue_When_ButtonIsClic
ked()
{
    var cut =
RenderComponent<CounterComponent>();

    var button = cut.Find("button");
    button.Click();

    Assert.Equal(1, cut.Instance.CurrentCount);
}
```

Here, a button click increments a counter value, and the test verifies that the CurrentCount property of the component reflects this change.

4. Mocking Dependencies:

When testing components that rely on external services or dependencies, it's important to mock these dependencies to isolate the component's logic. bUnit supports dependency injection, allowing you to inject mock services into your component tests.

Example: Mocking a Service

```
[Fact]
public void
WeatherComponent_Should_DisplayWeatherData_When
_ServiceReturnsData()
```

```
{
    // Arrange
    var mockWeatherService = new
Mock<IWeatherService>();
    mockWeatherService.Setup(s =>
s.GetWeatherAsync(It.IsAny<string>())).ReturnsA
sync("Sunny");

Services.AddSingleton<IWeatherService>(mockWeat
herService.Object);

    var cut =
RenderComponent<WeatherComponent>();

    // Act
    cut.Find("button").Click();

    // Assert
    cut.MarkupMatches("<div>Sunny</div>");
}
```

In this test, the IWeatherService is mocked to return predefined data, ensuring that the WeatherComponent can be tested independently of the actual service implementation.

Unit testing is a vital part of ensuring the quality and reliability of your Blazor components, particularly as they become more complex. Tools like bUnit provide a powerful framework for rendering components, simulating interactions, and verifying behavior in a test environment. By organizing your tests effectively and following best practices, you can ensure that your components are robust, maintainable, and ready for production. Whether you're testing simple UI elements or complex stateful components, unit tests help catch issues early, making your Blazor applications more stable and resilient.

Integration and UI Testing

While unit testing ensures that individual components function correctly in isolation, integration and UI testing validate that components work together as expected within the broader context of your application. These tests are crucial for catching issues that may arise from component interactions, routing, or state management across the application. In this section, we'll explore strategies for testing Blazor components within the full application context and discuss how to automate UI tests using tools like Selenium and Playwright.

Strategies for Testing Components within the Full Application Context

1. Integration Testing with bUnit and Blazor TestContext:

bUnit, in addition to unit testing, can also be used for integration testing within a Blazor application. You can use the Blazor `TestContext` to render components in a simulated environment that includes services, routing, and cascading parameters. This allows you to test how components behave when they interact with other parts of the application.

Example: Testing a Component with Routing and Services

```
using Bunit;
using Xunit;
using Microsoft.Extensions.DependencyInjection;
using MyBlazorApp.Services;
```

```csharp
public class ComponentIntegrationTests :
TestContext
{
    [Fact]
    public void
NavLink_Should_NavigateToCorrectPage_When_Click
ed()
    {
        // Arrange
        var mockNavManager =
Services.GetRequiredService<NavigationManager>(
);
        var cut =
RenderComponent<NavLink>(parameters =>
parameters
            .Add(p => p.Href, "/about")
            .Add(p => p.ChildContent,
"<span>About</span>")
        );

        // Act
        cut.Find("a").Click();

        // Assert
        Assert.Equal("/about",
mockNavManager.Uri);
    }
}
```

In this example, a `NavLink` component is tested to ensure that it navigates to the correct page when clicked. The test verifies that the NavigationManager correctly updates the URL after the click.

2. End-to-End Testing with Real Browsers:

End-to-end (E2E) testing involves testing your Blazor application in a real browser environment to simulate actual user behavior. This type of testing is critical for verifying that your application behaves as expected across different browsers and devices. E2E tests typically cover full user journeys, from interacting with the UI to verifying that the application responds correctly.

Example: End-to-End Testing Scenarios

- Verifying that the user can log in and navigate through the application.
- Testing form submissions and ensuring that the correct data is saved.
- Checking that dynamic content loads and updates correctly.

Automating UI Tests with Tools like Selenium or Playwright

Automating UI tests ensures that your application is continuously tested against a wide range of scenarios, reducing the risk of regressions when changes are made. Tools like Selenium and Playwright are popular choices for automating UI tests in Blazor applications.

1. Selenium:

Selenium is a widely-used tool for automating web browsers. It supports multiple programming languages, including C#, and can be used to write automated UI tests that simulate user interactions with your Blazor application.

Setting Up Selenium for Blazor Testing:

1. **Install Selenium WebDriver and ChromeDriver:**

```
dotnet add package Selenium.WebDriver
dotnet add package
Selenium.WebDriver.ChromeDriver
```

2. Write a Basic Selenium Test:

```
using OpenQA.Selenium;
using OpenQA.Selenium.Chrome;
using Xunit;

public class BlazorUITests
{
    [Fact]
    public void
BlazorApp_Should_DisplayHomePage()
    {
        using var driver = new
ChromeDriver();

driver.Navigate().GoToUrl("https://localh
ost:5001/");

        var header =
driver.FindElement(By.TagName("h1"));
        Assert.Equal("Welcome to My
Blazor App", header.Text);
    }
}
```

In this example, a Chrome browser is automated to navigate to the Blazor application's homepage and verify that the header text is correct. This test could be expanded to include interactions like clicking buttons, filling forms, and verifying navigation. Ensure you change the URl to your running application.

2. Playwright:

Playwright is a newer tool that supports testing across multiple browsers (Chrome, Firefox, and WebKit) with a unified API. It's particularly well-suited for testing modern web applications like those built with Blazor.

Setting Up Playwright for Blazor Testing:

1. **Install Playwright:**

   ```
   dotnet add package Microsoft.Playwright
   ```

2. **Write a Basic Playwright Test:**

   ```
   using System.Threading.Tasks;
   using Microsoft.Playwright;
   using Xunit;

   public class BlazorUITests
   {
       [Fact]
       public async Task
   BlazorApp_Should_DisplayHomePage()
       {
           using var playwright = await
   Playwright.CreateAsync();
           var browser = await
   playwright.Chromium.LaunchAsync(new
   BrowserTypeLaunchOptions { Headless =
   false });
           var page = await
   browser.NewPageAsync();
           await
   page.GotoAsync("https://localhost:5001/")
   ;

           var headerText = await
   page.InnerTextAsync("h1");
           Assert.Equal("Welcome to My
   Blazor App", headerText);
       }
   }
   ```

This example shows how to set up a Playwright test that launches a Chromium browser, navigates to the Blazor app, and verifies the header text. Playwright tests can be extended to cover complex user interactions and are particularly useful for cross-browser testing.

3. Running Automated Tests in CI/CD Pipelines:

Both Selenium and Playwright tests can be integrated into your Continuous Integration/Continuous Deployment (CI/CD) pipelines. This ensures that your Blazor application is automatically tested every time code is pushed or changes are made. Popular CI/CD tools like GitHub Actions, Azure DevOps, or Jenkins can be configured to run your automated UI tests as part of the build process, catching issues early before they reach production.

Integration and UI testing are crucial for ensuring that your Blazor application works correctly when all components interact within the full application context. By leveraging tools like bUnit for integration testing and Selenium or Playwright for UI testing, you can automate comprehensive tests that simulate real-world usage. These tests help you catch potential issues early, ensuring that your application is robust, user-friendly, and ready for deployment. Properly implemented testing strategies lead to higher-quality applications and a smoother user experience, making them an indispensable part of the Blazor development process.

Debugging Techniques

Debugging is an essential skill for any developer, especially when dealing with complex Blazor components. Blazor's combination of C#, .NET, and web technologies means that debugging can involve a mix of traditional server-side debugging practices and client-side web debugging techniques. This section covers effective debugging practices specific to Blazor components,

130

including the use of browser developer tools, logging, and tracing to diagnose and resolve complex issues.

Effective Debugging Practices Specific to Blazor Components

1. Leveraging Breakpoints and Step-Through Debugging:

Just like in any .NET application, you can set breakpoints in your Blazor components to pause execution and inspect the state of your application. Visual Studio and other .NET-compatible IDEs provide full debugging support for Blazor, allowing you to step through your C# code, inspect variables, and evaluate expressions.

Example: Setting Breakpoints in a Blazor Component

1. Open your Blazor project in Visual Studio.
2. Navigate to the `.razor` file containing the component you want to debug.
3. Click in the margin next to the line of code where you want to set a breakpoint.
4. Start the application in Debug mode (F5).

When the application runs and the execution hits the breakpoint, it will pause, allowing you to inspect variables and the call stack. You can step through the code using F10 (Step Over) or F11 (Step Into) to understand how the code is executed.

2. Debugging Blazor WebAssembly vs. Blazor Server:

Blazor WebAssembly (WASM) and Blazor Server have different debugging nuances:

- **Blazor WebAssembly:** Debugging is primarily client-side, meaning breakpoints and inspections happen in the browser. You can debug WebAssembly code directly in Visual Studio, but you also have the option to use browser developer tools.
- **Blazor Server:** Debugging is more akin to traditional ASP.NET Core applications, with breakpoints being hit on the server. However, because Blazor Server operates in real-time with SignalR, you need to ensure that the client and server states remain synchronized.

Using Browser Developer Tools, Logging, and Tracing for Complex Issues

1. Browser Developer Tools:

Browser developer tools are invaluable for debugging client-side issues in Blazor applications. These tools allow you to inspect the DOM, monitor network requests, view console output, and profile performance.

Inspecting the DOM:

- Use the Elements panel in your browser's developer tools to inspect the rendered HTML and CSS. This is particularly useful for verifying that your Blazor components are rendering correctly and that styles are being applied as expected.

Monitoring Network Requests:

- The Network panel helps you track HTTP requests made by your Blazor application. This is useful for debugging issues related to API calls, static assets, or any network-related errors.

Viewing Console Output:

- The Console panel displays any messages logged by your Blazor application using `Console.WriteLine`, `Console.Error`, or JavaScript `console.log()` statements. This can be helpful for debugging logic errors, uncaught exceptions, and more.

Example: Inspecting a Failed API Call

1. Open your Blazor application in the browser.
2. Press F12 to open the developer tools.
3. Navigate to the Network panel and filter by XHR to view API calls.
4. Click on a failed request to inspect the request and response details, including headers, status codes, and any error messages.

2. Using `ILogger` for Structured Logging:

Structured logging is a powerful technique for debugging complex Blazor components, particularly those that involve multiple services, asynchronous operations, or state management. The `ILogger` interface in Blazor allows you to log detailed messages, including variable values, execution paths, and error conditions.

Example: Adding Logging to a Blazor Component

```
@inject ILogger<WeatherComponent> Logger

<p>Weather: @weatherData</p>

@code {
```

```csharp
    private string weatherData = "Loading...";

    protected override async Task
OnInitializedAsync()
    {
        Logger.LogInformation("WeatherComponent
initialized");

        try
        {
            weatherData = await
FetchWeatherAsync();
            Logger.LogInformation("Weather data
fetched successfully");
        }
        catch (Exception ex)
        {
            Logger.LogError(ex, "Failed to
fetch weather data");
        }
    }

    private Task<string> FetchWeatherAsync()
    {
        // Simulate API call
        return Task.FromResult("Sunny, 25°C");
    }
}
```

In this example, `ILogger` is injected into the component, and log messages are recorded for the component's lifecycle events and data fetching process. If an error occurs during data fetching, the error and stack trace are logged.

3. Tracing with DiagnosticSource and EventSource:

For more in-depth analysis, you can use tracing with `DiagnosticSource` and `EventSource` to capture detailed diagnostic data. This is especially useful for diagnosing performance issues or tracking down hard-to-reproduce bugs.

Example: Using `DiagnosticSource` in a Service

```
public class WeatherService
{
    private readonly DiagnosticSource
_diagnosticSource;

    public WeatherService(DiagnosticSource
diagnosticSource)
    {
        _diagnosticSource = diagnosticSource;
    }

    public async Task<string> GetWeatherAsync()
    {

_diagnosticSource.Write("WeatherService.GetWeat
her.Start", new { });
        try
        {
            // Simulate API call
            await Task.Delay(500); // Simulate
delay

_diagnosticSource.Write("WeatherService.GetWeat
her.End", new { Weather = "Sunny, 25°C" });
            return "Sunny, 25°C";
        }
        catch (Exception ex)
        {

_diagnosticSource.Write("WeatherService.GetWeat
her.Error", new { Exception = ex });
            throw;
        }
    }
}
```

In this example, `DiagnosticSource` is used to write trace events for the start, end, and potential error during a weather data fetch operation. These events can be captured and analyzed using tools that listen for diagnostic events, helping you pinpoint where performance bottlenecks or errors occur.

Debugging Blazor components requires a combination of traditional .NET debugging techniques and web-specific tools. By effectively using breakpoints, browser developer tools, structured logging with `ILogger`, and tracing with `DiagnosticSource`, you can diagnose and resolve complex issues in your Blazor applications. These techniques not only help you identify and fix bugs more efficiently but also provide deeper insights into how your application behaves in different scenarios. Mastering these debugging practices is crucial for building reliable, high-performance Blazor applications that deliver a seamless user experience.

Chapter 8: Performance Optimization and Best Practices

As your Blazor applications grow in complexity, ensuring optimal performance becomes increasingly important. Poorly performing applications can lead to slow load times, laggy user interfaces, and a frustrating user experience. In this chapter, we will explore performance optimization techniques and best practices specifically tailored for Blazor applications. By understanding how to manage resources efficiently, minimize re-renders, and optimize data handling, you can build applications that are not only feature-rich but also fast and responsive. Whether you're developing small, interactive components or large-scale enterprise applications, these strategies will help you deliver a smooth and efficient user experience, keeping your Blazor applications performing at their best.

Profiling and Benchmarking Components

To ensure that your Blazor application runs efficiently, it's crucial to identify and resolve performance bottlenecks that can slow down the user experience. Profiling and benchmarking are essential practices for understanding how your components behave under different conditions and for pinpointing areas where optimization is needed. This section will cover tools and techniques for profiling Blazor applications and how to identify and address performance issues effectively.

Tools and Techniques for Profiling Blazor Applications

1. .NET Performance Profiler (Visual Studio):

Visual Studio provides a built-in .NET Performance Profiler that can be used to analyze Blazor Server applications. This tool helps you identify which parts of your application are consuming the most CPU, memory, and other resources.

Steps to Profile a Blazor Application:

1. **Open Your Project in Visual Studio:** Start by opening your Blazor project in Visual Studio.
2. **Select the Performance Profiler:** From the menu, navigate to `Debug > Performance Profiler` or press `Alt + F2`.
3. **Choose the Profiling Options:** In the Performance Profiler window, select the types of data you want to collect, such as CPU usage, memory allocation, and database interactions.
4. **Start Profiling:** Click `Start` to run your application and begin profiling. Use the application as you normally would to simulate real user interactions.
5. **Analyze the Results:** Once you've finished profiling, Visual Studio will display a detailed report showing where your application is spending the most time and which methods or components are the most resource-intensive. You can drill down into specific methods or code paths to identify potential bottlenecks.

2. Browser Developer Tools:

For Blazor WebAssembly applications, browser developer tools can be extremely useful for profiling and identifying performance issues. Most modern browsers, including Chrome, Edge, and Firefox, offer robust profiling tools.

Profiling with Chrome DevTools:

1. **Open Chrome DevTools:** Launch your Blazor application in Chrome and press `F12` to open DevTools.
2. **Navigate to the Performance Tab:** Click on the `Performance` tab to access the profiling tools.
3. **Record a Performance Profile:** Click `Record` and interact with your application to capture performance data. This might include navigating between pages, submitting forms, or performing actions that you suspect are slow.
4. **Analyze the Profile:** Once you stop recording, Chrome DevTools will provide a detailed breakdown of the performance data, including a timeline of events, CPU usage, and network activity. Look for areas where the application is spending excessive time, such as long-running JavaScript functions or excessive re-renders.

3. BenchmarkDotNet for Component-Level Benchmarking:

BenchmarkDotNet is a powerful .NET library that allows you to measure the performance of individual methods or components with high precision. It's particularly useful for benchmarking small, isolated pieces of code within your Blazor components.

Example: Benchmarking a Method in a Blazor Component

```
using BenchmarkDotNet.Attributes;
using BenchmarkDotNet.Running;

public class MyComponentBenchmark
```

```
{
    private MyComponent _component;

    [GlobalSetup]
    public void Setup()
    {
        _component = new MyComponent();
    }

    [Benchmark]
    public void RenderComponent()
    {
        _component.Render();
    }
}

public class Program
{
    public static void Main(string[] args)
    {
        var summary =
BenchmarkRunner.Run<MyComponentBenchmark>();
    }
}
```

In this example, BenchmarkDotNet is used to measure the performance of the `Render` method in a Blazor component. The results will provide detailed statistics on the method's execution time, helping you identify whether it's a performance bottleneck.

Identifying and Resolving Performance Bottlenecks

1. Minimize Component Re-renders:

Unnecessary re-renders can significantly impact the performance of your Blazor application. Use the `ShouldRender` method to control when a component should re-render, and avoid binding directly to properties that change frequently.

Example: Controlling Re-renders with ShouldRender

```
@code {
    private bool shouldRender;

    protected override bool ShouldRender()
    {
        return shouldRender;
    }

    private void UpdateState()
    {
        shouldRender = true;
        StateHasChanged();
    }
}
```

In this example, shouldRender is used to determine whether the component should re-render. This helps prevent unnecessary updates, particularly in complex UIs where frequent changes can degrade performance.

2. Optimize Data Loading and State Management:

Data loading and state management are common sources of performance bottlenecks, especially in applications that handle large datasets or rely heavily on real-time updates. Consider using techniques like lazy loading, virtualization, and efficient state management to reduce the impact of data operations on your application's performance.

Example: Using Virtualization for Large Data Sets

```
<Virtualize Items="@largeDataSet"
ItemSize="50">
```

```
    <ItemContent>
        @(context => <div>@context.Name</div>)
    </ItemContent>
</Virtualize>

@code {
    private List<Item> largeDataSet =
Enumerable.Range(1, 10000).Select(i => new Item
{ Name = $"Item {i}" }).ToList();
}
```

In this example, the `Virtualize` component is used to render only the visible items in a large data set, reducing the number of DOM elements and improving rendering performance. When using 3rd party components, ensure that the `Virtualize` component is support for the control.

3. Reduce JavaScript Interop Overhead:

While Blazor allows for JavaScript interop, excessive calls between C# and JavaScript can introduce latency and affect performance. Where possible, minimize the frequency and complexity of these interop calls, and prefer handling logic in C#.

Example: Consolidating JavaScript Interop Calls

```
[Inject] private IJSRuntime JSRuntime { get;
set; }

private async Task PerformBatchInterop()
{
    await
JSRuntime.InvokeVoidAsync("batchInterop", new
{ Action1 = "DoSomething", Action2 =
"DoSomethingElse" });
}
```

142

Instead of making multiple interop calls, this example consolidates them into a single batch operation, reducing the overhead of context switching between C# and JavaScript.

4. Monitor Memory Usage and Garbage Collection:

Memory leaks or excessive memory usage can lead to performance degradation over time. Use the profiling tools mentioned above to monitor memory allocations and garbage collection events, and optimize your components to release resources when they are no longer needed.

Example: Disposing Resources

```
@implements IDisposable

@code {
    private Timer _timer;

    protected override void OnInitialized()
    {
        _timer = new Timer(TimerCallback, null,
0, 1000);
    }

    public void Dispose()
    {
        _timer?.Dispose();
    }

    private void TimerCallback(object state)
    {
        // Timer logic
    }
}
```

In this example, the IDisposable interface is implemented to ensure that resources like timers are properly disposed of when the component is no longer in use, preventing memory leaks.

Profiling and benchmarking are critical practices for optimizing the performance of your Blazor components. By using tools like Visual Studio's Performance Profiler, browser developer tools, and BenchmarkDotNet, you can gain valuable insights into how your application behaves under different conditions. Identifying and resolving performance bottlenecks—whether related to re-renders, data loading, JavaScript interop, or memory usage— ensures that your Blazor applications remain fast, responsive, and efficient. These optimizations contribute to a better user experience and a more scalable application, making performance tuning an essential aspect of Blazor development.

Optimizing Render Performance

Rendering performance is crucial in Blazor applications, especially as components become more complex and interact with large datasets. Optimizing render performance involves reducing the time it takes for components to render and minimizing the number of updates to the DOM. This section will explore techniques for reducing component rendering times, minimizing DOM updates, and managing large data grids and virtualized lists effectively.

Techniques for Reducing Component Rendering Times and Minimizing DOM Updates

1. Avoid Unnecessary Re-renders:

One of the primary ways to optimize render performance is to prevent unnecessary re-renders of components. Blazor components re-render when their state changes, but not all state changes should trigger a re-render, especially if the visual output doesn't depend on the changed state.

Using `ShouldRender` to Control Rendering:

The `ShouldRender` method allows you to control whether a component should re-render. Override this method in your component to return `false` when a re-render is not required.

```
@code {
    private bool shouldRender = true;

    protected override bool ShouldRender()
    {
        return shouldRender;
    }

    private void UpdateState()
    {
        shouldRender = true;
        StateHasChanged();
    }

    private void SomeUnrelatedOperation()
    {
        shouldRender = false;
    }
}
```

In this example, `ShouldRender` is used to conditionally prevent the component from re-rendering unless explicitly required. This is particularly useful in scenarios where a state change doesn't affect the UI or when re-rendering would be expensive.

2. Use `@key` to Optimize List Rendering:

When rendering lists of items in Blazor, use the `@key` directive to improve rendering performance. The `@key` directive helps Blazor track each item's identity in the list, reducing the need for complex diffing algorithms and minimizing unnecessary DOM updates.

```
@foreach (var item in items)
{
    <div @key="item.Id">
        @item.Name
    </div>
}
```

By specifying a unique `@key` for each item, Blazor can optimize how it updates the DOM when the list changes. This is particularly beneficial in scenarios where the list frequently updates or where items are added and removed dynamically.

3. Break Down Large Components into Smaller, Reusable Ones:

Complex components that manage a lot of state or perform many operations during rendering can be broken down into smaller, more focused components. This modular approach not only improves maintainability but also allows Blazor to optimize the rendering of each small component individually.

Example: Breaking Down a Large Form Component

Instead of a single large form component:

```
<!-- LargeForm.razor -->
<form>
```

```
    <input @bind="Model.Name" />
    <input @bind="Model.Email" />
    <!-- many other fields -->
</form>
```

Consider breaking it down:

```
<!-- NameInput.razor -->
<input @bind="Model.Name" />

<!-- EmailInput.razor -->
<input @bind="Model.Email" />

<!-- MainForm.razor -->
<form>
    <NameInput Model="@Model" />
    <EmailInput Model="@Model" />
    <!-- other smaller components -->
</form>
```

Each subcomponent (NameInput, EmailInput, etc.) can be independently optimized and rendered, reducing the workload on the Blazor rendering engine and improving overall performance.

4. Minimize State Updates within the Component:

Frequent updates to component state can cause multiple re-renders, which can degrade performance. Instead of updating the state directly within the component logic, consider batching updates or updating the state only when necessary.

Example: Batching State Updates

```
@code {
    private int counter;

    private void IncrementCounter()
```

```
    {
        counter++;
        StateHasChanged(); // Only trigger re-
render after all updates
    }

    private void IncrementCounterByMultiple(int
increment)
    {
        counter += increment;
        StateHasChanged(); // Batch update
    }
}
```

In this example, `StateHasChanged` is only called after all updates are applied, reducing the number of re-renders and improving performance.

Strategies for Managing Large Data Grids and Virtualized Lists

1. Virtualization for Large Data Sets:

When dealing with large data grids or lists, rendering all items at once can significantly slow down your application. Virtualization is a technique that improves performance by only rendering the items that are currently visible in the viewport.

Using `Virtualize` Component for Virtualized Rendering:

Blazor provides a built-in `Virtualize` component that makes it easy to implement virtualization for large datasets.

```
<Virtualize Items="@largeDataSet"
ItemSize="50">
    <ItemContent>
        @(context => <div>@context.Name</div>)
```

```
        </ItemContent>
</Virtualize>

@code {
    private List<Item> largeDataSet =
Enumerable.Range(1, 10000).Select(i => new Item
{ Name = $"Item {i}" }).ToList();
}
```

In this example, only the visible items in `largeDataSet` are rendered, drastically reducing the number of DOM elements and improving both initial load times and scroll performance.

2. Efficient Data Loading with Paging:

For extremely large datasets, even virtualization might not be enough. Implementing data paging, where only a subset of data is loaded and displayed at any given time, can further enhance performance.

Example: Implementing Data Paging

```
@page "/paged-data"
@inject IDataService DataService

<div>
    <button
@onclick="PreviousPage">Previous</button>
    <button @onclick="NextPage">Next</button>

    <div>
        @foreach (var item in pagedData)
        {
            <div>@item.Name</div>
        }
    </div>
</div>

@code {
    private List<Item> pagedData;
```

```
    private int currentPage = 1;
    private int pageSize = 20;

    protected override async Task
OnInitializedAsync()
    {
        pagedData = await
LoadPageData(currentPage, pageSize);
    }

    private async Task<List<Item>>
LoadPageData(int page, int size)
    {
        return await
DataService.GetItemsAsync(page, size);
    }

    private async Task NextPage()
    {
        currentPage++;
        pagedData = await
LoadPageData(currentPage, pageSize);
    }

    private async Task PreviousPage()
    {
        if (currentPage > 1)
        {
            currentPage--;
            pagedData = await
LoadPageData(currentPage, pageSize);
        }
    }
}
```

This example loads data in pages, with `NextPage` and
`PreviousPage` buttons allowing the user to navigate
through the dataset. Only the data for the current page is
loaded and rendered, keeping the UI responsive.

3. Asynchronous Data Loading and Lazy Initialization:

When dealing with large grids or complex components, loading data asynchronously and using lazy initialization can prevent blocking the UI and improve perceived performance.

Example: Lazy Loading Data on Demand

```
@page "/lazy-data"
@inject IDataService DataService

<div>
    <button @onclick="LoadData">Load
Data</button>
    <div>
        @if (data != null)
        {
            @foreach (var item in data)
            {
                <div>@item.Name</div>
            }
        }
    </div>
</div>

@code {
    private List<Item> data;

    private async Task LoadData()
    {
        data = await
DataService.GetItemsAsync();
    }
}
```

Here, the data is loaded only when the user requests it (e.g., by clicking a button), rather than all at once. This approach can improve the initial load time of your application and ensure that only necessary data is fetched.

Optimizing render performance in Blazor involves a combination of strategies aimed at reducing the time it takes to render components and minimizing the number of DOM updates. By controlling re-renders, using virtualization for large datasets, and employing techniques like paging and lazy loading, you can build Blazor applications that are both responsive and efficient. These optimizations are essential for maintaining a smooth user experience, especially in applications that handle large amounts of data or complex UI elements. Implementing these best practices will help ensure that your Blazor applications perform well under various conditions, providing a superior experience for your users.

Best Practices for High-Performance Blazor Applications

Optimizing Blazor applications for performance is crucial, especially when targeting production environments. Blazor's rich feature set and modern development capabilities can lead to significant gains in productivity, but without attention to performance, applications may become sluggish, resulting in a poor user experience. This section provides a comprehensive guide to performance-oriented Blazor development, followed by a real-world case study on optimizing a Blazor application for production.

Comprehensive Guide to Performance-Oriented Blazor Development

1. **Component Design and Reusability**
   o **Keep Components Small and Focused:** Aim to create small, focused components. Large, monolithic components can be difficult to optimize and maintain. Breaking them down into smaller, reusable parts

allows for more granular performance tuning and easier debugging.

- o **Avoid Unnecessary Re-rendering:** Use the `ShouldRender` method or `@key` directive to control when components should re-render. This can prevent unnecessary UI updates, reducing the workload on the browser.
- o **Leverage `RenderFragment` and `EventCallback`:** Use `RenderFragment` for deferred rendering and `EventCallback` for efficient event handling, which helps in reducing the overhead associated with large components or complex event processing.

2. **Efficient Data Binding and State Management**
   - o **Optimize Data Binding:** Avoid complex expressions within data-binding syntax as these get executed multiple times during rendering. Instead, compute values in the code-behind or in lifecycle methods like `OnParametersSet`.
   - o **Use Asynchronous Programming:** Blazor supports asynchronous data binding and event handling. Use `async` and `await` to ensure that your UI remains responsive during long-running operations.
   - o **State Management Strategies:** Implement efficient state management using tools like `Fluxor` or `Blazor-State` to ensure that only the necessary components update when the state changes, reducing unnecessary re-renders.

3. **Lazy Loading and Bundling**
   - o **Lazy Load Components and Assemblies:** Utilize Blazor's support for lazy loading of components and assemblies to reduce the initial load time of your application. This

approach loads only the necessary parts of the application initially, improving perceived performance.

- o **Use Bundling and Minification:** Optimize static assets by bundling and minifying CSS and JavaScript files. This reduces the size of files that need to be downloaded, speeding up the initial load time.

4. **Optimizing Network Usage**
   - o **Efficient API Calls:** Batch API requests where possible and use `HttpClient` efficiently to avoid overloading the network with multiple small requests. Consider using `GraphQL` for more flexible and optimized data retrieval.
   - o **Leverage SignalR Wisely:** When using Blazor Server, optimize SignalR connections by reducing the frequency of real-time updates or using manual updates for less critical data, to lower the overhead on both server and client.

5. **Caching and Pre-rendering**
   - o **Use Caching Strategically:** Implement caching for static data and resources that don't change frequently. This can include in-memory caching, distributed caching (e.g., Redis), or browser-based caching strategies.
   - o **Pre-rendering:** Take advantage of Blazor's server-side pre-rendering capabilities to render pages on the server before sending them to the client. This reduces the perceived load time as users see content faster, even while the full Blazor WebAssembly application loads in the background.

6. **Performance Monitoring and Diagnostics**
   o **Profile Your Application:** Use tools like the browser's DevTools, .NET Core's diagnostic tools, and Application Insights to profile your application and identify performance bottlenecks.
   o **Logging and Telemetry:** Implement detailed logging and telemetry to monitor the performance of your application in production. This helps in quickly identifying and addressing performance issues.

Case Study: Optimizing a Blazor Application for Production

To illustrate the application of these best practices, let's examine a case study where a Blazor WebAssembly application was optimized for production use.

Scenario: A team was developing a Blazor WebAssembly application for an e-commerce platform. Initially, the application suffered from long load times, sluggish UI updates, and high memory usage, leading to a suboptimal user experience.

Steps Taken for Optimization:

1. **Component Optimization:**
   o The team started by analyzing the component structure and found several large components that handled multiple concerns. These components were refactored into smaller, reusable components. This not only improved maintainability but also allowed for more precise control over re-rendering, reducing the overall rendering time.

2. **Lazy Loading and Bundling:**
   o The application initially loaded all product categories and related data, leading to a bloated download size. The team implemented lazy loading for these components, ensuring that only the necessary categories were loaded initially. They also bundled and minified static assets, which reduced the size of CSS and JavaScript files by 40%.
3. **Network and API Optimization:**
   o The team optimized API calls by introducing batching for product data requests and implementing client-side caching for frequently accessed data. This reduced the number of API calls by 30% and improved the responsiveness of the application.
4. **State Management:**
   o A global state management solution was implemented using `Fluxor`. This allowed the team to control component updates more efficiently, ensuring that only components affected by state changes were re-rendered.
5. **Pre-rendering and Caching:**
   o Server-side pre-rendering was enabled for critical pages, significantly improving the time-to-first-byte (TTFB) and reducing perceived load times. Additionally, they implemented a caching strategy using Redis to store frequently accessed product data, reducing the load on the database.
6. **Performance Monitoring:**
   o Finally, the team set up Application Insights for real-time performance monitoring and diagnostics. This provided insights into

performance issues that occurred in production, allowing them to make further optimizations proactively.

Outcome: After implementing these optimizations, the application's load time improved by 50%, memory usage was reduced by 35%, and the overall user experience was significantly enhanced. The application could handle higher traffic without degradation in performance, resulting in a 20% increase in user retention.

This case study demonstrates the importance of following best practices and continuously monitoring and optimizing Blazor applications, especially when preparing for production environments. By applying the strategies discussed in this guide, developers can ensure their Blazor applications are not only feature-rich but also performant and scalable.

Chapter 9: Case Studies and Real-World Examples

In this chapter, we delve into the practical application of the concepts and techniques discussed throughout the book by exploring real-world case studies and examples. These case studies offer a deep dive into how Blazor has been leveraged across various industries to solve complex problems, improve user experiences, and drive business success. Each example is carefully chosen to demonstrate different aspects of Blazor development, from performance optimization and scalability to integrating with legacy systems and implementing cutting-edge features. By examining these real-world scenarios, you'll gain valuable insights and inspiration for applying Blazor in your own projects, ensuring that you're well-equipped to tackle the challenges of modern web development.

Case Study 1: Building a Customizable Data Grid Component

In this case study, we'll walk through the creation of a highly customizable data grid component in Blazor, complete with advanced features like sorting, filtering, and pagination. Data grids are a common requirement in enterprise applications, and building a feature-rich, performant grid can be challenging. This guide will provide a step-by-step approach to developing such a component, covering key design decisions, patterns, and best practices.

Step-by-Step Guide to Creating a Feature-Rich Data Grid

1. **Setting Up the Base Component**

- o **Component Structure:** Start by defining the base structure of the data grid component. This includes creating a parent component (`DataGrid.razor`) that will house the grid and its features. The parent component should expose parameters for the data source (`IEnumerable<T>`), column definitions, and grid configuration options like page size and initial sort order.
- o **Markup:** The basic HTML structure consists of a table element with `thead`, `tbody`, and optionally `tfoot` sections. For Blazor, use `@foreach` loops to dynamically generate rows and columns based on the data source and column definitions.
- o **Reusable Column Component:** Consider creating a `GridColumn` component that can be used to define the header, field, and formatting options for each column. This component will allow developers to specify how each column should behave without cluttering the main grid logic.

```
@typeparam TItem
<table class="table">
    <thead>
        <tr>
            @foreach (var column in
Columns)
            {
                <th>@column.Header</th>
            }
        </tr>
    </thead>
    <tbody>
        @foreach (var item in Items)
        {
            <tr>
```

```
                    @foreach (var column in
Columns)
                    {

<td>@column.CellTemplate(item)</td>
                    }
            </tr>
        }
    </tbody>
</table>
```

2. **Implementing Sorting**
    o   **Sortable Columns:** Add the ability to sort
        by clicking on the column headers. This
        requires an `OnSort` event handler that
        toggles the sort direction
        (ascending/descending) and applies the
        appropriate sort logic to the data source.
    o   **Sort Indicator:** Update the `GridColumn`
        component to include a sort indicator (e.g.,
        an arrow icon) that reflects the current sort
        direction. This provides visual feedback to
        users.
    o   **Sorting Logic:** Implement the sorting logic
        using LINQ. Depending on the data type,
        you may need to handle custom sorting
        scenarios, such as sorting by dates or
        numerical values differently from strings.

```
<th @onclick="() => OnSort(column)">
    @column.Header
    @if (SortColumn == column)
    {
        <span>@(SortDirection == "asc" ?
"▲" : "▼")</span>
    }
</th>
```

3. **Adding Filtering Capabilities**

160

- o **Filter UI:** Create a simple UI for filtering, such as input boxes or dropdowns, above the data grid. These should be linked to properties that store filter values for each column.
- o **Filter Logic:** Implement filtering logic that updates the displayed data based on the user's input. This can be done by applying a LINQ `Where` clause to the data source. Ensure that filtering is case-insensitive and can handle partial matches for text-based fields.
- o **Dynamic Filtering:** For larger datasets, consider implementing debounce functionality to prevent the grid from filtering with every keystroke, improving performance and user experience.

```
<input @bind="FilterValue"
placeholder="Filter..."
@oninput="ApplyFilter" />
@code {
    private void
ApplyFilter(ChangeEventArgs e)
    {
        FilteredItems = Items.Where(item
=> item.Name.Contains(FilterValue,
StringComparison.OrdinalIgnoreCase));
    }
}
```

4. **Implementing Pagination**
   - o **Pagination Controls:** Add pagination controls below the grid to allow users to navigate through pages of data. This includes buttons for moving to the next and previous pages, as well as an input or

dropdown for selecting the number of items per page.

- o **Paging Logic:** Implement the paging logic by slicing the data source based on the current page index and the selected page size. This can be achieved using LINQ's `Skip` and `Take` methods.
- o **Performance Considerations:** For large datasets, consider implementing server-side pagination, where only the necessary data for the current page is fetched from the server. This minimizes the data load and improves performance.

```
@code {
    private IEnumerable<TItem> PagedItems
=> Items.Skip((CurrentPage - 1) *
PageSize).Take(PageSize);

    private void OnPageChanged(int page)
    {
        CurrentPage = page;
    }
}
```

5. **Enhancing User Experience**
   - o **Responsive Design:** Ensure the data grid is responsive, adjusting the layout and visibility of columns based on screen size. This can be achieved using CSS media queries or a Blazor-based solution like `MudBlazor`.
   - o **Accessibility:** Implement accessibility features, such as ARIA attributes and keyboard navigation, to make the data grid usable for all users, including those with disabilities.

162

- o **Styling and Theming:** Provide options for customizing the appearance of the data grid, either through CSS classes or by exposing style parameters that can be adjusted by developers using the component.

Discussing the Design Decisions and Patterns Used

Building a customizable data grid component in Blazor involves several important design decisions and patterns that balance functionality, performance, and usability.

1. **Component Reusability and Modularity:**
   - o The decision to break down the grid into smaller, reusable components like `GridColumn` ensures that the grid remains modular and maintainable. Each piece of functionality (sorting, filtering, pagination) is encapsulated in its own component or method, following the Single Responsibility Principle.
2. **State Management:**
   - o Managing the state of sorting, filtering, and pagination in a Blazor component can be complex. In this case study, state is managed within the component itself, with properties like `SortColumn`, `FilterValue`, and `CurrentPage` driving the behavior of the grid. This keeps the logic contained and easy to test.
3. **Performance Considerations:**
   - o The implementation of features like lazy loading, debounce for filtering, and server-side pagination are critical for maintaining performance, especially when dealing with large datasets. The design prioritizes

performance by ensuring that only the necessary data is processed and rendered at any given time.

4. **User Experience and Accessibility:**
   o The user experience is enhanced through responsive design and accessibility features. These design choices ensure that the grid is not only functional but also user-friendly across different devices and for users with disabilities.

5. **Customization and Extensibility:**
   o By exposing parameters and events (e.g., for custom sorting logic or pagination handling), the grid is designed to be highly customizable. This allows developers to adapt the grid to a wide range of use cases without modifying the core component.

This case study highlights how careful planning and design can result in a powerful, customizable data grid component in Blazor. By following the steps outlined above and considering the discussed design decisions, developers can create feature-rich data grids that meet the needs of complex enterprise applications while maintaining high performance and a great user experience.

Case Study 2: Developing a Dynamic Form Builder

Dynamic form generation is a powerful feature that allows developers to create flexible, data-driven applications. In this case study, we will explore how to develop a dynamic form builder component in Blazor that can generate forms based on metadata. This includes handling complex scenarios like validation, state management, and dynamic layouts, ensuring that the form builder is both robust and user-friendly.

Creating a Form Builder Component That Dynamically Generates Forms Based on Metadata

1. **Defining the Metadata Structure**
   - **Form Metadata Model:** Begin by defining a model that represents the metadata for the form. This model will include details about the fields (e.g., field type, label, validation rules, and layout information). Each form field is represented by a `FormField` class, which contains properties like `Name`, `Label`, `FieldType`, `Required`, `Options` (for dropdowns or radio buttons), and `ValidationRules`.
   - **Dynamic Form Configuration:** Create a parent `DynamicForm` component that takes in this metadata and generates the form based on it. The metadata could be defined in code or fetched from an external source, such as an API or a configuration file.

```
public class FormField
{
    public string Name { get; set; }
    public string Label { get; set; }
    public string FieldType { get; set; }
// e.g., "text", "select", "checkbox"
    public bool Required { get; set; }
    public List<string> Options { get;
set; } // For dropdown or radio fields
    public string ValidationRules { get;
set; } // e.g., "required|min:3|max:100"
}
```

2. **Generating the Form Layout**
   - **Form Generation Logic:** In the `DynamicForm` component, use a loop to iterate over the list of `FormField` objects, dynamically generating the corresponding input fields. Blazor's templating features (`RenderFragment`) can be leveraged to create these fields dynamically based on the `FieldType` specified in the metadata.
   - **Dynamic Field Rendering:** For each field type (text input, dropdown, checkbox, etc.), create a method or a `RenderFragment` to render the appropriate UI element. For example, a text input field would use `<InputText>`, while a dropdown might use `<InputSelect>`.
   - **Conditional Layout:** Implement logic to arrange the fields according to the specified layout in the metadata. For instance, fields could be arranged in a grid, with different field types occupying varying amounts of space.

```
@typeparam TModel

@foreach (var field in Fields)
{
    <div class="form-group">
        <label
for="@field.Name">@field.Label</label>
        @if (field.FieldType == "text")
        {
            <InputText id="@field.Name"
class="form-control" @bind-
Value="Model.GetType().GetProperty(field.
Name).GetValue(Model)" />
        }
        else if (field.FieldType ==
"select")
```

```
        {
            <InputSelect id="@field.Name"
class="form-control" @bind-
Value="Model.GetType().GetProperty(field.
Name).GetValue(Model)">
                @foreach (var option in
field.Options)
                {
                    <option
value="@option">@option</option>
                }
            </InputSelect>
        }
        <!-- Additional field types here
-->
    </div>
}
```

3. **Handling Validation**
    o **Dynamic Validation Rules:** Utilize
      Blazor's built-in validation components like
      `EditForm`, `DataAnnotationsValidator`,
      and `ValidationMessage<T>` to handle form
      validation. The `ValidationRules` property
      from the metadata can be mapped to data
      annotations or custom validation logic.
    o **Custom Validation Logic:** For more
      complex validation scenarios, create custom
      validation attributes or logic within the
      `DynamicForm` component. This ensures that
      even dynamically generated forms adhere to
      specific business rules and constraints.
    o **Real-time Validation:** Implement real-time
      validation by triggering validation as users
      input data, providing instant feedback
      without requiring form submission. This can
      be achieved using `OnFieldChanged` events.

```
<EditForm Model="@Model"
OnValidSubmit="HandleValidSubmit">
    <DataAnnotationsValidator />
    @foreach (var field in Fields)
    {
        <div class="form-group">
            <label
for="@field.Name">@field.Label</label>
            @if (field.FieldType ==
"text")
            {
                <InputText
id="@field.Name" class="form-control"
@bind-
Value="Model.GetType().GetProperty(field.
Name).GetValue(Model)" />
                <ValidationMessage
For="@(() =>
Model.GetType().GetProperty(field.Name).G
etValue(Model))" />
            }
            <!-- Additional field types
here -->
        </div>
    }
    <button type="submit" class="btn btn-
primary">Submit</button>
</EditForm>
```

4. **State Management**
   o **Form State Handling:** Manage the state of
     the form using a Blazor component's state
     management features. The form data can be
     stored in a model object (TModel) that is
     bound to the form inputs. This model should
     be updated automatically as users interact
     with the form.
   o **Handling Complex Data Structures:** For
     forms that handle complex data structures
     (e.g., nested objects or collections), ensure
     that the state management logic can handle

168

these scenarios. This might involve iterating over nested metadata structures or using recursive methods to generate form sections.

- **Persisting Form State:** Implement mechanisms to persist form state between sessions, such as saving to local storage, server-side session storage, or a database. This is particularly useful for multi-step forms or when users need to save their progress.

5. **Implementing Dynamic Layouts**
   - **Responsive Layouts:** Design the DynamicForm component to support responsive layouts, allowing forms to adapt to different screen sizes. Use CSS grid or flexbox to implement dynamic layouts that rearrange fields based on screen width or metadata specifications.
   - **Conditional Sections:** Incorporate logic to show or hide form sections based on user input or predefined conditions. For example, certain fields might only appear if a specific option is selected in another field. This can be controlled by adding conditional rendering logic in the Blazor template.

```
<div class="dynamic-form">
    @foreach (var section in
FormSections)
    {
        if (section.ConditionMet(Model))
        {
            <fieldset>

<legend>@section.Title</legend>
                @foreach (var field in
section.Fields)
                {
```

```
                          <div class="form-
group">
                              <!-- Render field
as before -->
                          </div>
                      }
                  </fieldset>
              }
          }
      </div>
```

6. **User Experience Enhancements**
   o **Progress Indicators:** For multi-step forms, add progress indicators to show users where they are in the process. This can be implemented using a progress bar or step indicators that update as users navigate through the form.
   o **Accessibility Considerations:** Ensure that the dynamic form builder is accessible by using semantic HTML and appropriate ARIA roles. Include keyboard navigation and screen reader support to make the forms usable by all users.
   o **Custom Styling and Theming:** Allow customization of form styles and themes through parameters or CSS class bindings. This enables developers to integrate the dynamic form builder seamlessly into various application designs.

Discussing the Design Decisions and Patterns Used

Building a dynamic form builder in Blazor requires thoughtful design decisions to ensure flexibility, maintainability, and ease of use. Let's explore the key design choices made in this case study:

1. **Metadata-Driven Design:**
   - The choice to base form generation on metadata allows for a high degree of flexibility. This approach decouples the form structure from the code, making it easier to update and extend the form without altering the underlying codebase. It also enables the dynamic creation of forms based on external data sources, such as configuration files or API responses.
2. **Component Modularity:**
   - By breaking down the form builder into smaller, reusable components (like `DynamicForm`, `FormField`, and input templates), the design adheres to the Single Responsibility Principle. Each component focuses on a specific aspect of the form, making the code easier to manage and test.
3. **State and Validation Management:**
   - The use of Blazor's built-in validation and state management features ensures that the dynamic form builder maintains a consistent and reliable user experience. The ability to handle complex data structures and validation scenarios is crucial for real-world applications, where forms often require nuanced and conditional logic.
4. **Customizability and Extensibility:**
   - The design emphasizes customizability by allowing developers to define custom validation rules, layout structures, and styling options. This ensures that the form builder can be tailored to meet the specific needs of different applications, whether it's a simple contact form or a complex multi-step process.

5. **Performance Considerations:**
   - Performance is maintained by minimizing re-renders and efficiently managing state updates. The design also allows for lazy loading of form sections and real-time validation without overloading the browser, ensuring that the form builder remains responsive even in complex scenarios.
6. **User Experience Focus:**
   - The inclusion of features like responsive layouts, conditional rendering, and accessibility support ensures that the dynamic form builder provides a seamless and inclusive user experience. These design choices are critical for building forms that are not only functional but also user-friendly and accessible to a wide audience.

This case study highlights how Blazor's powerful component model can be used to build a dynamic form builder that is both flexible and robust. By following the steps and design patterns outlined above, developers can create dynamic forms that adapt to a variety of use cases, ensuring high usability and maintainability in their applications.

Case Study 3: Implementing a Dashboard with Reusable Widgets

Dashboards are critical components in many applications, providing users with real-time insights through visual data representations. In this case study, we'll explore how to design and implement a Blazor-based dashboard featuring modular, draggable, and resizable widgets. We'll also cover techniques for handling real-time data updates and ensuring responsive design, making the dashboard both powerful and adaptable to various user needs.

Designing a Dashboard with Modular, Draggable, and Resizable Widgets

1. **Setting Up the Base Dashboard Structure**
   - **Dashboard Layout Component:** Start by creating a `Dashboard.razor` component that serves as the main container for the dashboard. This component will be responsible for managing the layout and positioning of widgets. The layout can be structured using CSS Grid or Flexbox to facilitate drag-and-drop functionality and responsive behavior.
   - **Widget Model:** Define a `Widget` model that includes properties such as `Id`, `Title`, `Content`, `Position`, `Size`, and any necessary configuration options. Each widget will be represented by a Blazor component that renders the widget's content and manages its state.
   - **Widget Container:** Create a `DashboardWidget` component that encapsulates the logic for each widget. This component will handle the rendering of the widget's header (title, controls) and body (content), as well as drag-and-drop and resizing functionality.

```
public class Widget
{
    public string Id { get; set; }
    public string Title { get; set; }
```

```
    public RenderFragment Content { get;
set; }
    public string Position { get; set; }
// E.g., "grid-row: 1; grid-column: 1 /
span 2;"
    public string Size { get; set; } //
E.g., "width: 400px; height: 300px;"
}
razor
@typeparam TWidget

<div class="dashboard-widget"
style="@Widget.Position @Widget.Size">
    <div class="widget-header">
        <h3>@Widget.Title</h3>
        <!-- Controls for dragging,
resizing, etc. -->
    </div>
    <div class="widget-body">
        @Widget.Content
    </div>
</div>
```

2. **Implementing Drag-and-Drop Functionality**
   o **Drag-and-Drop Support:** Utilize
     HTML5's drag-and-drop API in
     combination with Blazor's event handling to
     enable users to reposition widgets within the
     dashboard. This requires handling
     `onmousedown`, `ondragstart`, `ondrag`, and
     `ondrop` events to track the widget's position
     and update the layout dynamically.
   o **Grid-Based Layout System:** Implement a
     grid-based layout system using CSS Grid.
     This approach allows for easy placement
     and alignment of widgets. As widgets are
     dragged, their grid positions should update
     in real-time, snapping to the nearest grid cell
     when dropped.

- o **Persisting Layout State:** Save the widget positions and sizes to local storage or a database to ensure that users' custom layouts persist between sessions. This can be managed by serializing the `Widget` model and saving it via JavaScript interop or Blazor's `LocalStorage` support.

```
@code {
    private void
OnDragStart(DragEventArgs e, Widget
widget)
    {

e.DataTransfer.SetData("widgetId",
widget.Id);
    }

    private void OnDrop(DragEventArgs e)
    {
        var widgetId =
e.DataTransfer.GetData("widgetId");
        // Update widget position based
on drop location
    }
}
```

3. **Enabling Resizable Widgets**
   - o **Resizable Borders:** Add resize handles to the edges of each `DashboardWidget` component. These handles can be simple `div` elements that users can click and drag to resize the widget. Handle `onmousedown`, `onmousemove`, and `onmouseup` events to adjust the widget's size dynamically as it is resized.
   - o **Resize Logic:** Implement the resizing logic by updating the `Size` property of the `Widget` model. Ensure that resizing is constrained to

175

prevent widgets from overlapping or extending beyond the dashboard boundaries.

- o **Responsive Resizing:** Make sure the resizing respects the grid system, snapping to grid lines where appropriate. This ensures that widgets maintain a consistent layout and alignment with other dashboard elements.

```
<div class="resize-handle"
@onmousedown="StartResize"></div>

@code {
    private void
StartResize(MouseEventArgs e)
    {
        // Implement resizing logic
    }
}
```

4. **Handling Real-Time Data Updates**
   - o **SignalR for Real-Time Data:** Use SignalR to push real-time data updates to the dashboard widgets. Each `DashboardWidget` component can subscribe to specific SignalR hubs that provide the data updates it needs. This allows the dashboard to display live data, such as stock prices, metrics, or other dynamic content.
   - o **Efficient Data Handling:** Implement efficient data handling to minimize the impact of frequent updates on performance. This may involve throttling updates, only rendering changes when necessary, or using a background service to aggregate data before pushing updates to the UI.
   - o **Updating Widgets in Real-Time:** Within each widget component, handle incoming data updates by updating the component's

176

state and triggering a re-render. Use `InvokeAsync(StateHasChanged)` to ensure that updates are processed correctly within Blazor's rendering pipeline.

```
@code {
    private void
HandleDataUpdate(DataUpdate update)
    {
        // Update the widget's state and
trigger a re-render
        InvokeAsync(StateHasChanged);
    }
}
```

5. **Ensuring Responsive Design**
   - **Responsive Layouts:** Design the dashboard to be fully responsive, ensuring that it looks and works well on a variety of screen sizes, from desktops to mobile devices. Use media queries to adjust the grid layout and widget sizes based on the screen width.
   - **Adaptive Widgets:** Make individual widgets adapt their content and layout based on available space. This could involve simplifying the content, collapsing elements, or changing the visualization type (e.g., switching from a bar chart to a line chart) when the widget is resized or viewed on smaller screens.
   - **Mobile Touch Support:** Implement touch support for dragging, dropping, and resizing widgets on mobile devices. Use touch events in Blazor (`ontouchstart`, `ontouchmove`, `ontouchend`) to handle interactions that would normally be managed with a mouse on desktop.

```
@media (max-width: 768px) {
    .dashboard-widget {
        width: 100%;
        height: auto;
    }
}
```

Techniques for Handling Real-Time Data Updates and Responsive Design

Creating a dashboard that effectively handles real-time data updates while maintaining a responsive design involves several key techniques:

1. **Efficient Data Handling with SignalR:**
   - Real-time dashboards require frequent updates to display the latest data. By using SignalR, you can push updates from the server to the client in real-time, ensuring that the dashboard remains current. However, frequent updates can strain both the server and the client, so it's essential to implement efficient data handling techniques, such as throttling updates or batching data changes before applying them to the UI.
2. **State Management and Optimization:**
   - Managing the state of a dashboard with multiple widgets can be complex, especially when each widget requires its own real-time data stream. Efficient state management ensures that the dashboard performs well even under heavy load. Use Blazor's `RenderFragment` and `StateHasChanged` methods judiciously to control when and how the UI updates in response to state changes.
3. **Responsive Design Patterns:**

o A responsive dashboard should adjust not only the layout of widgets but also their content and behavior based on the device or screen size. This requires implementing responsive design patterns such as CSS Grid and media queries, along with adaptive UI components that can change their presentation based on available space. For example, a widget displaying a detailed chart might switch to a simplified version on smaller screens.

4. **Touch Interaction Support:**
   o Ensuring that the dashboard is fully functional on touch devices is critical for mobile users. Implementing touch interaction support for dragging, dropping, and resizing widgets ensures that the dashboard remains intuitive and easy to use on tablets and smartphones. This involves handling touch events and providing visual feedback that is appropriate for touch interfaces, such as larger drag handles and tap-friendly controls.

5. **Persisting User Customizations:**
   o Users often customize dashboards to fit their specific needs, so it's important to persist these customizations between sessions. Techniques such as saving layout configurations to local storage or synchronizing with a backend database can provide a seamless experience where users' layouts and preferences are automatically restored whenever they return to the application.

Discussing the Design Decisions and Patterns Used

Building a dashboard with modular, draggable, and resizable widgets in Blazor involves several critical design decisions and patterns:

1. **Componentization for Reusability:**
   o The dashboard is composed of modular `DashboardWidget` components, each encapsulating its own logic, layout, and data handling. This component-based architecture not only promotes reusability but also makes it easier to manage and extend the dashboard's functionality.

2. **Grid-Based Layout for Flexibility:**
   o The choice of a grid-based layout system (using CSS Grid) allows for flexible positioning and resizing of widgets. This approach simplifies the implementation of drag-and-drop functionality while ensuring that the layout remains organized and consistent across different screen sizes.

3. **Real-Time Data Integration:**
   o Integrating SignalR for real-time data updates ensures that the dashboard is always up-to-date, providing users with the most current information. The design balances performance and responsiveness by optimizing how and when data updates are processed and rendered.

4. **Responsive and Adaptive Design:**
   o The dashboard is designed to be fully responsive, ensuring usability on a wide range of devices. Adaptive design techniques allow widgets to adjust their content and layout dynamically, ensuring

that the dashboard remains functional and visually appealing on both large screens and mobile devices.

5. **User-Centric Customization:**
   o The ability to drag, drop, resize, and customize widgets empowers users to tailor the dashboard to their specific needs. Persisting these customizations across sessions enhances the user experience by providing continuity and convenience.

This case study demonstrates how Blazor's component model and real-time capabilities can be harnessed to create a dynamic, user-friendly dashboard. By following the techniques and design patterns outlined above, developers can build dashboards that are not only powerful and feature-rich but also responsive and adaptable to various user needs and device types.

Chapter 10: Publishing and Sharing Blazor Component Libraries

In this chapter, we explore the final stages of Blazor component development: publishing and sharing your component libraries. Creating reusable components is a powerful way to accelerate development and maintain consistency across applications, but to truly maximize their value, it's essential to distribute them effectively. We will guide you through the process of packaging your Blazor components into a library, publishing them to NuGet, and sharing them with the community or your organization. Additionally, we'll cover best practices for versioning, documentation, and ensuring your components are ready for public use. By the end of this chapter, you'll have the knowledge to not only build robust Blazor components but also to make them available to developers everywhere.

Packaging and Distributing Components

Packaging and distributing your Blazor components as reusable libraries allows you to share your work with the broader developer community or within your organization, ensuring that others can easily integrate your components into their projects. This section will walk you through the best practices for packaging components, setting up NuGet packages, and managing dependencies effectively.

Best Practices for Packaging Components as Reusable Libraries

1. **Organizing Your Component Library**
   o **Modular Structure:** Organize your component library into a clear, modular structure that makes it easy for developers to

navigate and use. Each component should reside in its own folder, with related files (e.g., `.razor` files, CSS, JavaScript, and images) grouped together. This approach not only improves maintainability but also makes it easier for users to understand and integrate your components.

- **Namespace Conventions:** Use consistent and descriptive namespace conventions for your components. Namespaces should reflect the structure and purpose of your library, making it clear where each component belongs. For example, a library called `MyCompany.UI` might have namespaces like `MyCompany.UI.Buttons` or `MyCompany.UI.Modals`.

- **Documentation:** Include XML comments in your component code to generate documentation automatically. Well-documented components help users understand how to use them correctly and reduce the learning curve for new adopters.

```
namespace MyCompany.UI.Buttons
{
    /// <summary>
    /// Represents a customizable button
component with various styles and
behaviors.
    /// </summary>
    public partial class MyButton :
ComponentBase
    {
        // Component logic here
    }
}
```

2. **Creating a Project for Your Component Library**
   o **Blazor Class Library Project:** Use a Blazor class library project (`.NET Standard` or `.NET Core`) to package your components. This type of project is optimized for creating reusable Blazor components and allows you to include all necessary resources, such as static files and JavaScript interop, in a single package.
   o **Multi-Targeting for Compatibility:** Consider multi-targeting your library to support different versions of .NET and Blazor, ensuring broader compatibility with various projects. This can be done by specifying multiple target frameworks in your `.csproj` file.

```
<Project Sdk="Microsoft.NET.Sdk.Razor">
  <PropertyGroup>

<TargetFrameworks>net7.0;netstandard2.1</
TargetFrameworks>
  </PropertyGroup>
</Project>
```

3. **Bundling Static Assets**
   o **Include Static Assets:** If your components rely on static assets such as CSS, JavaScript, or images, ensure these are bundled correctly within the library. Blazor class libraries allow you to include static files that can be automatically referenced in projects that use your library.
   o **Content Directory:** Place your static assets in the `wwwroot` directory of your library project. When the library is packaged, these assets will be included and can be

referenced by the consuming application using a relative path.

```
<ItemGroup>
  <EmbeddedResource
Include="wwwroot\**\*.*" />
</ItemGroup>
```

4. **Versioning Your Components**
   o **Semantic Versioning:** Adopt semantic versioning (SemVer) for your component library, using version numbers in the format Major.Minor.Patch (e.g., 1.0.0). This helps communicate the nature of changes between releases, where major versions introduce breaking changes, minor versions add backward-compatible features, and patch versions include bug fixes.
   o **Changelog Maintenance:** Maintain a detailed changelog that documents changes, fixes, and new features in each release. This is essential for users to understand the impact of upgrading to a new version of your library.

```
<PropertyGroup>
    <Version>1.0.0</Version>
</PropertyGroup>
```

Setting Up NuGet Packages and Managing Dependencies

1. **Creating and Configuring a NuGet Package**
   o **NuGet Package Metadata:** Configure your library's .csproj file with the necessary metadata for creating a NuGet package. This includes the package ID, version, authors,

license information, and a brief description of what the library offers.

```xml
<PropertyGroup>
    <PackageId>MyCompany.UI</PackageId>
    <Version>1.0.0</Version>
    <Authors>Your Name</Authors>
    <Description>A Blazor component
library for building UI
elements.</Description>

<PackageLicenseExpression>MIT</PackageLic
enseExpression>

<PackageProjectUrl>https://github.com/you
rrepo</PackageProjectUrl>

<RepositoryUrl>https://github.com/yourrep
o</RepositoryUrl>
    <PackageIcon>icon.png</PackageIcon>

<PackageTags>blazor;ui;components</Packag
eTags>
</PropertyGroup>
```

- o **Build and Pack:** Use the `dotnet pack` command to generate a NuGet package from your library. This command bundles your component library, including all necessary assets, into a `.nupkg` file that can be published to NuGet.org or a private NuGet server.

```
dotnet pack -c Release
```

2. **Managing Dependencies**
   - o **Include Required Dependencies:** Ensure that your library's dependencies are correctly specified in the `.csproj` file. For example, if your components rely on

specific Blazor or .NET libraries, these should be listed as package references. This ensures that users of your library automatically pull in the necessary dependencies when they install your package.

```
<ItemGroup>
    <PackageReference
Include="Microsoft.AspNetCore.Components.
Web" Version="7.0.0" />
    <PackageReference
Include="SomeOtherLibrary"
Version="1.2.3" />
</ItemGroup>
```

- o **Dependency Conflicts:** Be mindful of potential dependency conflicts that might arise when your library is used alongside others. Test your library in a variety of project setups to identify and mitigate issues, such as incompatible package versions or transitive dependencies that could cause conflicts.
3. **Publishing the NuGet Package**
   - o **Publishing to NuGet.org:** If you want to share your component library with the public, you can publish it to NuGet.org. First, create an account on NuGet.org and generate an API key. Then, use the `dotnet nuget push` command to upload your `.nupkg` file to NuGet.org.

```
dotnet nuget push YourPackage.nupkg -k
YourApiKey -s
https://api.nuget.org/v3/index.json
```

- o **Private NuGet Servers:** For internal distribution, consider using a private NuGet server or a service like Azure Artifacts. This allows you to share your library within your organization while keeping it private. Configure the package source in your `.csproj` or NuGet.config files to point to your private server.

```
<PropertyGroup>

<RestoreSources>https://mycompany.com/nug
et/v3/index.json</RestoreSources>
</PropertyGroup>
```

4. **Testing and Quality Assurance**
   - o **Automated Testing:** Implement automated tests for your components using a test project in your solution. This ensures that your components work as expected across different scenarios. Use tools like xUnit, MSTest, or NUnit to write unit tests and integration tests.
   - o **Continuous Integration:** Set up a continuous integration (CI) pipeline to automatically build, test, and package your component library whenever changes are made. Services like GitHub Actions, Azure Pipelines, or GitLab CI/CD can help automate these processes, ensuring that your library is always in a releasable state.

```
name: Build and Test
on: [push]
jobs:
  build:
    runs-on: ubuntu-latest
    steps:
```

```
- uses: actions/checkout@v2
- name: Set up .NET
  uses: actions/setup-dotnet@v1
  with:
    dotnet-version: '7.0.x'
- name: Install dependencies
  run: dotnet restore
- name: Build
  run: dotnet build --configuration
Release
- name: Run tests
  run: dotnet test --no-build --
verbosity normal
```

By following these best practices for packaging and distributing your Blazor components, you ensure that your libraries are well-organized, easy to use, and accessible to other developers. Whether you're sharing your components with the public via NuGet.org or distributing them internally within your organization, careful planning and attention to detail in packaging, dependency management, and testing will help you deliver high-quality, reliable component libraries.

Documentation and API Design

Creating a successful Blazor component library involves more than just writing functional code; it requires careful attention to documentation and API design. Effective documentation ensures that users can quickly understand and utilize your components, while a well-designed API provides a consistent and intuitive interface that makes your library easy to adopt and integrate into other projects. In this section, we'll cover best practices for creating comprehensive documentation and designing user-friendly APIs for your Blazor component library.

Creating Effective Documentation for Your Component Library

1. **Comprehensive Overview**
   - **Introduction and Getting Started:** Start your documentation with an overview that introduces your component library, its purpose, and its key features. Include a "Getting Started" section that walks users through the steps to install and configure the library in their Blazor projects. Provide clear examples that demonstrate basic usage, helping users quickly get up and running.

```
# MyCompany.UI Library

The `MyCompany.UI` library is a
collection of reusable Blazor components
designed to streamline UI development.
With components ranging from buttons to
complex data grids, this library helps
you build rich, interactive web
applications quickly.

## Getting Started

### Installation

To install the library, use the NuGet
Package Manager Console:
```

Install-Package MyCompany.UI

```
Copy code

Alternatively, add it to your project
file:
```

```xml
<PackageReference Include="MyCompany.UI"
Version="1.0.0" />
```

Basic Example

Here's a quick example of how to use the `MyButton`
component:

```
<MyButton Text="Click Me"
OnClick="HandleClick" />
```

2. **Component-Specific Documentation**
   o **Detailed Component Descriptions:** For
     each component in your library, provide
     detailed documentation that includes the
     purpose of the component, its properties,
     methods, events, and how it integrates with
     other components. Use code snippets and
     examples to illustrate how each feature
     works in practice.

```
## MyButton Component

The `MyButton` component is a versatile
button that supports different styles,
sizes, and click events. It's designed to
be easily customizable while providing
consistent behavior across your
application.

### Properties

- `Text`: The text displayed on the
button.
  - Type: `string`
  - Default: `""`

- `IsPrimary`: Whether the button uses
the primary color scheme.
```

```
- Type: `bool`
- Default: `false`
```

Events

```
- `OnClick`: Triggered when the button is
clicked.
  - Type: `EventCallback<MouseEventArgs>`
```

Example

```razor
<MyButton Text="Save" IsPrimary="true"
OnClick="SaveData" />
```

3. **Usage Examples and Scenarios**
   o **Real-World Examples:** Include real-world usage examples that show how to combine different components from your library to solve common UI challenges. This not only helps users understand the capabilities of your library but also provides them with practical solutions that they can adapt to their own projects.

```markdown
## Real-World Example: Form with
Validation
```

```
Here's an example of using `MyInput` and
`MyButton` components to create a form
with validation:
```

```razor
<EditForm Model="@formData"
OnValidSubmit="HandleValidSubmit">
    <DataAnnotationsValidator />

    <MyInput Label="Name" @bind-
Value="formData.Name" />
    <ValidationMessage For="@(() =>
formData.Name)" />
```

```
    <MyInput Label="Email" @bind-
Value="formData.Email" />
    <ValidationMessage For="@(() =>
formData.Email)" />

    <MyButton Text="Submit"
IsPrimary="true" />
</EditForm>

@code {
    private FormData formData = new
FormData();

    private void HandleValidSubmit()
    {
        // Submit form data
    }
}
```

4. **API Reference and XML Comments**
   - **API Reference Generation:** Use tools like
     DocFX or Sandcastle to generate a
     comprehensive API reference from XML
     comments in your code. This should include
     detailed descriptions of all public classes,
     methods, properties, and events in your
     library.
   - **Consistent XML Comments:** Ensure that
     all public members of your components are
     documented with XML comments. These
     comments should be clear, concise, and
     provide information about the purpose and
     usage of each member.

```
/// <summary>
/// Represents a customizable button
component with various styles and
behaviors.
```

```
/// </summary>
/// <param name="Text">The text displayed
on the button.</param>
/// <param name="IsPrimary">Whether the
button uses the primary color
scheme.</param>
/// <param name="OnClick">Event triggered
when the button is clicked.</param>
public partial class MyButton :
ComponentBase
{
    [Parameter]
    public string Text { get; set; }

    [Parameter]
    public bool IsPrimary { get; set; }

    [Parameter]
    public EventCallback<MouseEventArgs>
OnClick { get; set; }
}
```

5. **Interactive Documentation and Samples**
   - **Interactive Demos:** Consider creating an interactive documentation site using a tool like Blazor WASM that allows users to try out components directly in the browser. Interactive demos help users experiment with your components and see the effects of different properties and settings in real-time.
   - **Sample Projects:** Provide sample projects that users can clone and run locally. These projects should demonstrate typical use cases for your components and include well-commented code to help users understand how everything fits together.

```
## Sample Project
```

```
Clone the
[MyCompany.UI.Sample](https://github.com/
yourrepo/MyCompany.UI.Sample) repository
to see examples of how to use the
components in a real application.

bash
Copy code
git clone
https://github.com/yourrepo/MyCompany.UI.
Sample.git
```

Designing Intuitive and Consistent APIs for End-Users

1. **Simplicity and Usability**
   - **Intuitive Defaults:** Design your components with sensible defaults that make them easy to use out of the box. Developers should be able to drop a component into their application with minimal configuration and still get useful functionality.
   - **Consistency Across Components:** Ensure that similar components follow consistent naming conventions and behaviors. For instance, if multiple components have an OnClick event, it should always be named the same way and behave consistently across all components.

```
public partial class MyButton :
ComponentBase
{
    // Properties and events follow
consistent patterns
    [Parameter]
    public string Text { get; set; } =
"Click Me";
```

```
    [Parameter]
    public EventCallback<MouseEventArgs>
OnClick { get; set; }
}
```

2. **Flexibility and Extensibility**
   o **Parameterization:** Allow users to customize your components through parameters that control various aspects of their appearance and behavior. Provide flexibility without overwhelming users with too many options. Ensure that complex features are optional and only need to be configured when required.
   o **Event Handling and Callbacks:** Design your API to expose key events and callbacks, enabling developers to hook into the component's lifecycle and extend its functionality. For example, components like data grids should provide events for sorting, filtering, and data changes.

```
public partial class MyDataGrid<TItem> :
ComponentBase
{
    [Parameter]
    public IEnumerable<TItem> Items
{ get; set; }

    [Parameter]
    public EventCallback<SortEventArgs>
OnSort { get; set; }

    // Additional parameters and events
}
```

3. **API Consistency and Naming Conventions**

- o **Clear Naming Conventions:** Use clear and descriptive names for properties, methods, and events that align with established conventions in the .NET ecosystem. Avoid abbreviations and ensure that names accurately describe the functionality they represent.
- o **Consistent Method Signatures:** Maintain consistency in method signatures across components. For example, if a method requires an `EventCallback<T>` in one component, similar methods in other components should follow the same pattern.

```
public partial class MyModal :
ComponentBase
{
    [Parameter]
    public bool IsVisible { get; set; }

    [Parameter]
    public EventCallback OnClose { get;
set; }

    public void Open()
    {
        IsVisible = true;
    }

    public void Close()
    {
        IsVisible = false;
        OnClose.InvokeAsync();
    }
}
```

4. **Error Handling and Feedback**
   - o **Graceful Error Handling:** Design your components to handle errors gracefully and

provide meaningful feedback to users. For example, if a component fails to load data from an API, it should display an error message instead of crashing.

o **Validation and User Input:** Provide built-in validation for user input, ensuring that components fail early and informatively if they are misconfigured or used incorrectly. Use exceptions and error messages that clearly indicate what went wrong and how to fix it.

```
public partial class MyInput :
ComponentBase
{
    [Parameter]
    public string Value { get; set; }

    [Parameter]
    public EventCallback<string>
ValueChanged { get; set; }

    protected override void
OnParametersSet()
    {
        if (string.IsNullOrEmpty(Value))
        {
            throw new
ArgumentException("Value cannot be null
or empty.", nameof(Value));
        }
    }
}
```

5. **Future-Proofing and Deprecation Strategies**
   o **Versioning API Changes:** When making changes to your API, especially breaking changes, ensure that you increment the major version number according to semantic

versioning principles. Clearly document the changes and provide guidance on how users can update their code.

o **Deprecation Warnings:** If you need to deprecate a feature or method, provide deprecation warnings with clear instructions for migrating to the new API. Allow for a transition period where both the old and new APIs are available, giving users time to adapt.

```
[Obsolete("Use MyButton with the
'IsPrimary' parameter instead.")]
public partial class OldButton :
ComponentBase
{
    // Old implementation
}
```

Focusing on comprehensive documentation and intuitive API design ensures that your Blazor component library is not only powerful but also accessible and easy to use. These practices help developers quickly understand your components and integrate them into their projects, ultimately leading to broader adoption and greater success for your library.

Open Source and Community Contributions

The open-source community around Blazor is vibrant and growing, providing an invaluable resource for developers looking to build powerful, flexible web applications. Contributing to this community not only helps you improve your skills and knowledge but also allows you to give back by sharing your work with others. In this section, we'll explore how you can contribute to and benefit from the

Blazor open-source community, followed by a case study on successfully releasing an open-source Blazor component library.

How to Contribute to and Benefit from the Blazor Open-Source Community

1. **Getting Started with Open Source**
   - **Understand the Ecosystem:** Begin by familiarizing yourself with the Blazor open-source ecosystem. Explore popular Blazor projects on GitHub, such as Blazorise, MudBlazor, and the official Blazor repository. Understanding the landscape will help you identify gaps or areas where you can contribute.
   - **Start Small:** If you're new to open source, start by contributing to existing projects. Look for issues labeled as "good first issue" or "help wanted." These issues are often more approachable and provide a great way to get involved. Contributing documentation, bug fixes, or small features are excellent starting points.

```
# Contributing to Blazorise

Thank you for your interest in
contributing to Blazorise! We welcome
contributions of all kinds, including bug
fixes, feature enhancements, and
documentation improvements. Here's how
you can get started:

1. **Fork the repository** and clone it
locally.
2. **Create a new branch** for your
changes.
```

```
3. **Make your changes** and ensure all
tests pass.
4. **Submit a pull request** with a
detailed description of your changes.
```

2. **Contributing Code and Features**
   - **Forking and Cloning Repositories:** To
     contribute to a Blazor project, fork the
     repository to your GitHub account and clone
     it to your local machine. This allows you to
     make changes independently of the main
     project.
   - **Creating Pull Requests:** After making your
     changes, create a pull request (PR) to
     propose your changes to the main
     repository. Make sure your PR includes a
     clear description of what you've done and
     why, along with any relevant issue
     references. Be responsive to feedback from
     maintainers and be prepared to iterate on
     your PR if necessary.
   - **Following Coding Standards:** Adhere to
     the coding standards and guidelines
     provided by the project. This includes
     writing clean, well-documented code,
     following the project's naming conventions,
     and including tests where applicable.
     Consistency with the existing codebase is
     crucial for your contributions to be accepted.

```
# Pull Request Guidelines

- **Title and Description:** Make sure
your PR title is descriptive and your
description clearly explains what the PR
does.
```

```
- **Linked Issues:** If your PR addresses
an issue, link it in the description
(e.g., "Fixes #123").
- **Testing:** Ensure all tests pass
before submitting your PR. If you've
added new features, include tests for
them.
```

3. **Documentation and Community Engagement**
    o **Contributing Documentation:** Good
      documentation is vital to the success of
      open-source projects. You can contribute by
      improving existing documentation, adding
      new tutorials, or writing guides on specific
      use cases. This is especially valuable for
      new users who may struggle to understand
      how to use the project without clear
      documentation.
    o **Answering Questions and Providing
      Support:** Participate in the community by
      answering questions on platforms like
      GitHub Discussions, Stack Overflow, and
      Gitter. Helping others not only strengthens
      the community but also deepens your own
      understanding of Blazor.
    o **Proposing Ideas and Enhancements:** If
      you have ideas for new features or
      enhancements, propose them to the
      community. Most projects welcome
      suggestions that can improve the library.
      Use GitHub Issues or Discussions to outline
      your proposal and gather feedback from
      maintainers and other users.

```
# How to Contribute Documentation

- **Improve Existing Docs:** Review the
current documentation for accuracy,
```

clarity, and completeness. Submit
improvements as pull requests.
- **Write New Guides:** If you notice
gaps in the documentation, consider
writing new guides or tutorials. Topics
might include advanced usage scenarios,
integration with other tools, or best
practices.
- **Community Engagement:** Help answer
questions from other users in the
community forums or on GitHub
Discussions. Your insights can be
invaluable to those just starting out
with Blazor.

4. **Maintaining Your Own Open-Source Project**
   o **Starting a New Project:** If you have
     developed a Blazor component library or
     tool that could benefit others, consider
     releasing it as an open-source project.
     Ensure it is well-documented, thoroughly
     tested, and has a clear license (e.g., MIT or
     Apache 2.0) that defines how others can use
     and contribute to it.
   o **Building a Community:** Actively maintain
     your project by responding to issues,
     reviewing pull requests, and regularly
     updating the codebase. Encourage
     community contributions by providing clear
     contribution guidelines and fostering a
     welcoming environment. Over time, your
     project may grow into a significant part of
     the Blazor ecosystem.
   o **Versioning and Releases:** Use semantic
     versioning to manage your project's
     releases. Publish new versions regularly,
     especially when major updates or fixes are
     introduced. Communicate changes

effectively through release notes and changelogs.

```
# My Blazor Component Library

Welcome to My Blazor Component Library!
This project provides a collection of
reusable Blazor components designed to
simplify your web development process.

## Contributing

We welcome contributions from the
community! Whether you're fixing a bug,
adding a new feature, or improving
documentation, your help is greatly
appreciated.

- **Reporting Issues:** If you find a
bug, please [open an
issue](https://github.com/yourrepo/issues
).
- **Submitting Changes:** Fork the
repository, make your changes in a new
branch, and submit a pull request.
- **License:** This project is licensed
under the MIT License.
```

Case Study: Releasing an Open-Source Blazor Component Library

Background: Let's consider the case of "BlazorWidgets", a fictional open-source Blazor component library designed to provide a set of customizable UI widgets for web applications. The project began as an internal tool at a small software development company but was later released as an open-source library to contribute to the Blazor community.

Step 1: Preparing for Open Source

- The development team at the company recognized that the widgets they had built could be useful to other developers. Before releasing the library, they spent time refactoring the code to ensure it was clean, well-documented, and modular. They also wrote comprehensive tests to cover all the key functionalities.

Step 2: Licensing and Initial Setup

- The team chose the MIT License for their project to maximize accessibility and encourage contributions. They created a GitHub repository for BlazorWidgets and uploaded the code along with the necessary project files, including a `README.md`, `LICENSE`, and `CONTRIBUTING.md` to guide new users and contributors.

Step 3: Documentation and Examples

- To make the library easy to use, the team created a detailed `README.md` that included an overview of the project, installation instructions, and basic usage examples. They also added a `/docs` folder with more in-depth guides and an example project that users could clone to see the widgets in action.

Step 4: Community Engagement

- After the initial release, the team actively promoted the project on social media, Blazor forums, and developer communities. They also answered questions, responded to issues, and welcomed feedback from the community. Over time, the project gained traction, and other developers began contributing to it.

Step 5: Managing Contributions

- As contributions started coming in, the team put in place a CI/CD pipeline to automatically build and test all pull requests. They also established a code review process to ensure that all changes met their quality standards. This process helped maintain the integrity of the library as it grew.

Step 6: Regular Updates and Releases

- The team followed a regular release schedule, using semantic versioning to communicate the nature of updates (e.g., `1.0.0`, `1.1.0`, `2.0.0`). They published detailed release notes for each version, highlighting new features, bug fixes, and any breaking changes. This transparency helped users manage their dependencies effectively.

Outcome: BlazorWidgets became a popular library within the Blazor community, used by developers worldwide to build rich, interactive web applications. The project's success was largely due to the team's commitment to quality, documentation, and community engagement. By releasing their work as open source, they not only contributed valuable tools to the community but also benefited from the collective input and improvements made by others.

Key Takeaways:

- **Start with a Solid Foundation:** Ensure your project is clean, well-documented, and tested before releasing it as open source.
- **Engage with the Community:** Actively participate in the community by answering questions, reviewing contributions, and fostering a welcoming environment.
- **Maintain and Evolve:** Regularly update your project, communicate changes clearly, and keep improving based on user feedback.

This case study illustrates the potential impact of contributing to the Blazor open-source community and the benefits of sharing your work with others. Whether you're contributing to existing projects or starting your own, engaging with the open-source ecosystem can be a rewarding experience that helps you grow as a developer while benefiting the community at large.

Chapter 11: Conclusion

As we conclude our journey through Blazor development, it's essential to recap the key concepts we've explored and look ahead to the future of Blazor UI development. Blazor is a powerful framework that continues to evolve, offering developers exciting opportunities to build modern, interactive web applications with .NET. In this final chapter, we'll summarize the main points covered throughout the book and discuss emerging trends and technologies in the Blazor ecosystem. We'll also reflect on the importance of continuous learning and staying updated with Blazor as it progresses.

Recap of Key Concepts

Chapter 1: Introduction to Blazor

- **Blazor Overview:** We introduced Blazor as a powerful framework for building interactive web applications using .NET, focusing on its ability to run client-side in the browser via WebAssembly or server-side with Blazor Server.
- **Blazor WebAssembly vs. Blazor Server:** The key differences between Blazor WebAssembly and Blazor Server were outlined, including their respective use cases, performance considerations, and deployment models.
- **Getting Started:** We provided a quick start guide to setting up a Blazor project, covering the necessary tools and the basic structure of a Blazor application.

Chapter 2: Building Blazor Components

- **Component Basics:** We explored the core building blocks of Blazor—components. This chapter covered how to create, structure, and use components, along with the principles of component-based architecture.
- **Lifecycle Methods:** The component lifecycle methods (`OnInitialized`, `OnParametersSet`, `OnAfterRender`, etc.) were discussed in detail, emphasizing their role in managing component state and behavior.
- **Event Handling:** We covered event handling in Blazor, showing how to bind events such as clicks to methods in your components, and how to pass data through events.

Chapter 3: Data Binding and State Management

- **Data Binding:** We delved into data binding techniques, including one-way (`@bind-Value`) and two-way data binding, highlighting how these are used to synchronize UI elements with underlying data models.
- **State Management:** Various state management strategies were explored, from simple stateful components using local variables to more complex scenarios involving cascading parameters, `StateContainer` services, and external state management libraries like Fluxor.

Chapter 4: Forms and Validation

- **Creating Forms:** This chapter focused on building forms in Blazor, covering standard input components like `InputText`, `InputSelect`, and custom input components.

- **Validation Techniques:** We discussed form validation using Blazor's `DataAnnotationsValidator`, custom validation attributes, and third-party libraries to ensure user inputs meet specified criteria.

Chapter 5: Advanced Blazor Features

- **JavaScript Interop:** The chapter explored how to extend Blazor's functionality by interacting with JavaScript through JavaScript interop, allowing developers to call JavaScript functions from C# and vice versa.
- **Performance Optimization:** We provided strategies for optimizing Blazor applications, focusing on reducing initial load times, managing memory, and improving UI responsiveness through techniques like lazy loading and pre-rendering.
- **Third-Party Integration:** This section showed how to integrate third-party libraries and tools into Blazor applications, enhancing their capabilities with minimal effort.

Chapter 6: Testing and Debugging Blazor Applications

- **Unit Testing Blazor Components:** We discussed best practices for writing unit tests for Blazor components using testing frameworks like xUnit and bUnit.
- **Debugging Techniques:** The chapter covered various debugging techniques, including using browser developer tools, Visual Studio's debugging features, and logging to diagnose and fix issues in Blazor applications.

Chapter 7: Deploying Blazor Applications

- **Deployment Strategies:** We examined different deployment strategies for Blazor applications, including deployment to static web hosts for Blazor WebAssembly and configuring web servers for Blazor Server.
- **CI/CD Integration:** The chapter highlighted the importance of integrating continuous integration and continuous deployment (CI/CD) pipelines to automate the build, test, and deployment processes for Blazor applications.

Chapter 8: Case Studies and Real-World Examples

- **Building a Data Grid:** We walked through a case study on building a customizable data grid component, showcasing features like sorting, filtering, and pagination.
- **Dynamic Form Builder:** This case study focused on creating a dynamic form builder in Blazor, demonstrating how to generate forms based on metadata, manage state, and handle validation dynamically.
- **Dashboard with Reusable Widgets:** We explored the creation of a modular, draggable, and resizable dashboard, including techniques for handling real-time data updates and ensuring responsive design.

Chapter 9: Publishing and Sharing Blazor Component Libraries

- **Packaging Components:** We covered the best practices for packaging Blazor components as reusable libraries, including structuring your project, bundling static assets, and ensuring compatibility across different .NET versions.

- **Setting Up NuGet Packages:** The chapter provided a step-by-step guide to creating and publishing NuGet packages, managing dependencies, and maintaining version control for your Blazor component libraries.
- **Documentation and API Design:** We emphasized the importance of creating comprehensive documentation and designing intuitive APIs, ensuring that your libraries are easy to use and integrate.

Chapter 10: Open Source and Community Contributions

- **Contributing to Open Source:** This chapter explored how to contribute to the Blazor open-source community, including participating in existing projects, proposing new features, and submitting pull requests.
- **Releasing Open-Source Libraries:** We presented a case study on releasing an open-source Blazor component library, discussing the key steps involved in preparing, publishing, and maintaining an open-source project.

This recap highlights the breadth and depth of topics covered in this book. Each chapter builds on the previous ones, providing you with a comprehensive understanding of Blazor and the tools to succeed in developing robust, scalable web applications. As you continue to explore and apply these concepts, you will become more proficient in leveraging Blazor to its full potential.

Looking Forward: The Future of Blazor UI Development

As the Blazor ecosystem continues to grow and evolve, it's essential to stay informed about emerging trends and technologies that will shape the future of Blazor UI development. This section explores some of these trends, highlighting how they are poised to impact the way developers build web applications using Blazor. We'll also discuss the importance of continuous learning and staying updated with the latest developments in Blazor, ensuring you remain at the forefront of this rapidly advancing field.

Emerging Trends and Technologies in the Blazor Ecosystem

1. **Blazor Hybrid Applications**
   - **Blazor and .NET MAUI Integration:** One of the most exciting developments in the Blazor ecosystem is the rise of Blazor Hybrid applications, which combine Blazor with .NET MAUI (Multi-platform App UI). This integration allows developers to create cross-platform applications that run on Windows, macOS, Android, and iOS, using a single Blazor codebase. Blazor Hybrid apps leverage the power of native device capabilities while maintaining the flexibility of web development, making it a compelling choice for developers looking to target multiple platforms with minimal effort.
   - **Desktop and Mobile Applications:** Blazor Hybrid opens up new opportunities for building desktop and mobile applications that share components with web applications. This trend is likely to grow, as

developers seek to unify their codebases and reduce the overhead of maintaining separate code for web, mobile, and desktop environments.

2. **WebAssembly Advancements**
   - **Performance Improvements:** WebAssembly (WASM), the technology that powers Blazor WebAssembly, continues to see significant advancements. Upcoming improvements in WebAssembly include better support for multi-threading, SIMD (Single Instruction, Multiple Data) operations, and faster startup times. These enhancements will make Blazor WebAssembly even more performant, enabling it to handle more complex and demanding applications.
   - **Broader Browser Support:** As WebAssembly becomes more mature and widely adopted, browser support continues to improve. This broader support ensures that Blazor WebAssembly applications run smoothly across all major browsers, including mobile browsers, further solidifying its position as a viable option for high-performance web applications.

3. **Component Ecosystem Growth**
   - **Rich Component Libraries:** The Blazor component ecosystem is rapidly expanding, with a growing number of open-source and commercial component libraries available. These libraries offer pre-built UI components, such as charts, grids, and forms, that developers can easily integrate into their applications. The continued growth of these libraries will reduce

development time and help developers deliver feature-rich applications more quickly.

- o **Custom Component Development:** As more developers adopt Blazor, the demand for custom components tailored to specific industries or use cases will increase. This trend will likely lead to the creation of specialized component libraries that cater to niche markets, further enriching the Blazor ecosystem.

4. **Serverless and Microservices Integration**
   - o **Blazor with Serverless Architectures:** The integration of Blazor with serverless architectures is another trend to watch. Serverless platforms like Azure Functions and AWS Lambda allow developers to build scalable, event-driven applications without managing server infrastructure. Blazor can act as the front-end for these serverless backends, providing a seamless and highly scalable user experience.
   - o **Microservices and Blazor:** As microservices continue to gain traction, Blazor applications are increasingly being used as the front-end for microservices-based backends. This approach allows developers to build modular, scalable applications that can easily adapt to changing business requirements. Blazor's flexibility in consuming APIs and integrating with various backend services makes it an ideal choice for microservices architectures.

5. **Enhanced Tooling and IDE Support**

- Improved Developer Experience: The Blazor development experience is continually being enhanced with better tooling and IDE support. Visual Studio, Visual Studio Code, and Rider are adding new features tailored specifically for Blazor, such as improved debugging, enhanced IntelliSense, and more powerful design-time tools. These improvements help streamline the development process and increase productivity.
- Testing and Debugging Tools: The availability of advanced testing and debugging tools for Blazor is also growing. Tools like bUnit for unit testing Blazor components, and improved browser debugging capabilities, are making it easier for developers to test and debug their applications, ensuring higher quality code and faster iteration cycles.

Final Thoughts on Continuous Learning and Staying Updated with Blazor

1. Embrace Continuous Learning
   - Staying Current: The technology landscape, particularly within the Blazor ecosystem, is constantly evolving. To stay competitive and make the most of Blazor's capabilities, it's crucial to engage in continuous learning. Follow official updates from Microsoft, read blogs, watch tutorials, and participate in online courses to keep your skills sharp and up-to-date.
   - Experimentation: Don't be afraid to experiment with new features and

approaches. Blazor is a flexible and evolving framework, and experimenting with it can lead to innovative solutions and a deeper understanding of its capabilities. Whether it's trying out a new component library or exploring a different architectural pattern, hands-on experimentation is a powerful way to learn.

2. **Engage with the Community**
   o **Community Involvement:** The Blazor community is a vibrant and supportive network of developers. Engage with this community by participating in forums, contributing to open-source projects, and attending conferences and meetups. These interactions not only provide opportunities to learn from others but also to share your knowledge and experience, fostering a collaborative environment.
   o **Contributing to Open Source:** As you gain experience with Blazor, consider contributing back to the community. Whether it's through code contributions, writing tutorials, or answering questions on forums, your involvement can help others and strengthen the Blazor ecosystem. Contributing to open-source projects also enhances your skills and builds your reputation as a knowledgeable and helpful developer.

3. **Adapt to Change**
   o **Embracing New Paradigms:** As Blazor and related technologies evolve, new paradigms and best practices will emerge. Being adaptable and willing to embrace these changes is key to staying relevant and

effective in your development career. Stay open to learning new tools, adopting new workflows, and rethinking your approach as the ecosystem evolves.

- ○ **Future-Proofing Your Skills:** Investing in your continuous learning and professional development is essential for future-proofing your career. By staying informed about the latest trends and technologies, you can position yourself as a forward-thinking developer who is prepared to tackle the challenges of tomorrow.

Final Words

Blazor represents a significant advancement in web development, enabling .NET developers to build rich, interactive applications with ease. As you continue to explore and apply the concepts discussed in this book, you'll be well-prepared to leverage Blazor's full potential in your projects. By staying committed to continuous learning, engaging with the community, and adapting to new trends, you'll ensure that you remain at the forefront of Blazor UI development, ready to create innovative solutions in an ever-changing digital landscape.

Sample Code and Repositories

This appendix provides a collection of sample code snippets and links to repositories that are valuable resources for Blazor developers. These examples cover a wide range of scenarios, from basic component creation to more advanced use cases like state management, JavaScript interop, and performance optimization. Additionally, the listed repositories are excellent starting points for exploring real-world Blazor applications and gaining hands-on experience.

These sample code snippets and repositories provide practical examples of how to implement various features in Blazor. By exploring these examples, you can gain a deeper understanding of how to build robust, scalable Blazor applications. Feel free to clone the repositories, experiment with the code, and adapt the examples to your own projects. As you continue your Blazor journey, these resources will serve as valuable references and learning tools.

Sample Code Snippets

1. **Basic Blazor Component**
   o A simple Blazor component demonstrating basic data binding and event handling.

```
@page "/counter"
@code {
    private int currentCount = 0;

    private void IncrementCount()
    {
        currentCount++;
    }
}
```

```
<h3>Counter</h3>

<p>Current count: @currentCount</p>

<button class="btn btn-primary"
@onclick="IncrementCount">Click
me</button>
```

2. Form with Validation

- o A Blazor form that uses data annotations for validation.

```
@page "/form"
@using
System.ComponentModel.DataAnnotations

@code {
    private UserModel user = new
UserModel();

    private void HandleValidSubmit()
    {
        // Handle valid form submission
    }

    private class UserModel
    {
        [Required(ErrorMessage = "Name is
required")]
        public string Name { get; set; }

        [EmailAddress(ErrorMessage =
"Invalid email address")]
        [Required(ErrorMessage = "Email
is required")]
        public string Email { get; set; }
    }
}

<EditForm Model="@user"
OnValidSubmit="HandleValidSubmit">
    <DataAnnotationsValidator />
```

```
    <div class="form-group">
        <label>Name:</label>
        <InputText class="form-control"
@bind-Value="user.Name" />
        <ValidationMessage For="@(() =>
user.Name)" />
    </div>

    <div class="form-group">
        <label>Email:</label>
        <InputText class="form-control"
@bind-Value="user.Email" />
        <ValidationMessage For="@(() =>
user.Email)" />
    </div>

    <button type="submit" class="btn btn-
primary">Submit</button>
</EditForm>
```

3. **JavaScript Interop Example**
   o Demonstrating JavaScript interop in Blazor by calling a JavaScript function from C#.

```
@page "/interop"
@inject IJSRuntime JS

@code {
    private async Task ShowAlert()
    {
        await JS.InvokeVoidAsync("alert",
"Hello from Blazor!");
    }
}

<h3>JavaScript Interop</h3>

<button class="btn btn-secondary"
@onclick="ShowAlert">Show Alert</button>

<script>
    function showAlert(message) {
        alert(message);
```

```
        }
</script>
```

4. **State Management with Cascading Parameters**
   o Using cascading parameters to share state
     across components.

```
@page "/cascading"

@code {
    private AppState state = new
AppState();
}

<CascadingValue Value="@state">
    <ParentComponent />
</CascadingValue>

@code {
    public class AppState
    {
        public int Counter { get; set; }
= 0;
    }
}
razor
@code {
    [CascadingParameter]
    public AppState State { get; set; }

    private void Increment()
    {
        State.Counter++;
    }
}

<h4>Parent Component</h4>

<button
@onclick="Increment">Increment</button>
<p>Counter: @State.Counter</p>

<ChildComponent />
```

```
@code {
    [CascadingParameter]
    public AppState State { get; set; }
}

<h4>Child Component</h4>
<p>Counter in child: @State.Counter</p>
```

5. **Component with RenderFragment**
   - A reusable component that accepts a
     `RenderFragment` to allow custom content.

```
@code {
    [Parameter]
    public RenderFragment ChildContent
{ get; set; }
}

<div class="custom-card">
    <h4>Card Title</h4>
    <div class="card-body">
        @ChildContent
    </div>
</div>
razor
Copy code
@page "/renderfragment"

<CustomCard>
    <p>This is the content inside the
card!</p>
</CustomCard>
```

Sample Repositories

1. **Blazing Pizza Workshop**
   - **Link:** <u>Blazing Pizza</u>
   - **Description:** This repository is part of the
     official Microsoft Blazor workshop. It
     demonstrates how to build a real-world
     Blazor WebAssembly app from scratch,

complete with server-side APIs and SignalR integration for real-time updates.

2. **BlazorHero Clean Architecture**
   - **Link:** BlazorHero
   - **Description:** BlazorHero is a boilerplate project built with Blazor WebAssembly and .NET Core 5.0. It follows the Clean Architecture principles and includes advanced features like role-based authentication, a rich UI with MudBlazor, and more.

3. **MudBlazor Component Library**
   - **Link:** MudBlazor
   - **Description:** MudBlazor is a popular UI component library built on Blazor. It provides a wide range of ready-to-use components that follow Material Design principles, making it easier to build visually appealing Blazor applications.

4. **Blazor Boilerplate**
   - **Link:** Blazor Boilerplate
   - **Description:** This repository provides a starter template for Blazor applications, featuring a modular architecture, authentication, authorization, and API integration. It's a good starting point for building enterprise-level Blazor apps.

5. **BlazorStrap**
   - **Link:** BlazorStrap
   - **Description:** BlazorStrap is a Bootstrap 4 & 5 component library for Blazor. It allows you to easily integrate Bootstrap-styled components into your Blazor application, enhancing the UI without writing extensive CSS.

6. **CarChecker - An End-to-End Blazor Sample**

- o **Link:** CarChecker
- o **Description:** CarChecker is an end-to-end sample application built with Blazor WebAssembly. It showcases several advanced Blazor features, including PWA (Progressive Web App) support, offline capabilities, and API integration.

7. **Blazor RealWorld Example**
   - o **Link:** Blazor RealWorld
   - o **Description:** A Blazor implementation of the RealWorld example app. This repository provides a full-stack, real-world application built with Blazor, featuring authentication, CRUD operations, and more.

8. **eShopOnWeb Blazor UI**
   - o **Link:** eShopOnWeb Blazor
   - o **Description:** This project is part of Microsoft's eShopOnWeb reference architecture, demonstrating how to build a fully functional e-commerce site using Blazor alongside other .NET technologies.

9. **TimeWarp - A Blazor Fluxor Example**
   - o **Link:** TimeWarp
   - o **Description:** A project that demonstrates using the Fluxor state management library with Blazor to build a time-traveling app. It's a great resource for learning how to manage complex state in Blazor applications.

10. **BlazorCalendar - A Blazor Event Calendar**
    - o **Link:** BlazorCalendar
    - o **Description:** This repository showcases how to build an event calendar using Blazor. It includes features like event creation, editing, and deletion, making it a useful

reference for building calendar-based applications.

Blazor Syntax Cheat Sheet

This cheat sheet provides a quick reference to the most common Blazor syntax, lifecycle methods, and component patterns. Keep it handy while you develop Blazor applications to streamline your workflow and ensure you're following best practices.

1. Component Basics

- **Component Declaration:**

```
@page "/example"       // Defines a route
for the component
@using MyNamespace     // Imports a
namespace

<h3>Hello, @Name!</h3>  // Razor syntax
for binding

@code {
    private string Name = "World";  // C#
code block
}
```

- **Passing Parameters:**

```
@code {
    [Parameter]
    public string Title { get; set; }
}

<h1>@Title</h1>
```

- **Event Handling:**

```
razor
<button @onclick="IncrementCount">Click
me</button>
```

```
@code {
    private int count = 0;

    private void IncrementCount()
    {
        count++;
    }
}
```

2. Data Binding

- **One-Way Data Binding:**

```
<p>@message</p>

@code {
    private string message = "Hello,
Blazor!";
}
```

- **Two-Way Data Binding:**

```
<input @bind="name" />

@code {
    private string name;
}
```

- **Binding with Format:**

```
<input @bind="price" @bind:format="C" />

@code {
    private decimal price = 19.99M;
}
```

3. Conditional Rendering

- **if/else Statements:**

```
@if (isLoggedIn)
{
    <p>Welcome back!</p>
}
else
{
    <p>Please log in.</p>
}

@code {
    private bool isLoggedIn = true;
}
```

- **foreach Loop:**

```
<ul>
    @foreach (var item in items)
    {
        <li>@item</li>
    }
</ul>

@code {
    private string[] items = { "Apple",
"Banana", "Cherry" };
}
```

4. Lifecycle Methods

- **OnInitialized:** Invoked when the component is initialized.

```
@code {
    protected override void
OnInitialized()
    {
        // Initialization logic here
    }
}
```

- **OnParametersSet:** Called when the component's parameters have been set or updated.

```
@code {
    protected override void
OnParametersSet()
    {
        // Handle parameter updates
    }
}
```

- **OnAfterRender:** Called after the component has finished rendering.

```
@code {
    protected override void
OnAfterRender(bool firstRender)
    {
        if (firstRender)
        {
            // Do something on first
render
        }
    }
}
```

5. Component Patterns

- **Child Components:**

```
<ChildComponent Title="Hello from Parent"
/>

@code {
    [Parameter]
    public string Title { get; set; }
}
```

- **Cascading Parameters:**

```
<CascadingValue Value="@appState">
```

```
    <ChildComponent />
</CascadingValue>

@code {
    private AppState appState = new
AppState();

    public class AppState
    {
        public string StateValue { get;
set; } = "Shared State";
    }
}
```

Child Component:

```
@code {
    [CascadingParameter]
    public AppState AppState { get;
set; }
}

<p>State value: @AppState.StateValue</p>
```

- **EventCallback:**

```
<ChildComponent OnClick="HandleClick" />

@code {
    private void HandleClick()
    {
        // Event handling logic
    }
}

// Child Component
@code {
    [Parameter]
    public EventCallback OnClick { get;
set; }

    private async Task TriggerClick()
    {
```

```
    await OnClick.InvokeAsync();
    }
}
```

6. Routing

- **Defining a Route:**

```
@page "/route"

<h3>Welcome to the route!</h3>
```

- **Route with Parameters:**

```
@page "/route/{id:int}"

@code {
    [Parameter]
    public int Id { get; set; }
}

<p>Route parameter ID: @Id</p>
```

7. Dependency Injection

- **Injecting a Service:**

```
@inject HttpClient Http

@code {
    private string data;

    protected override async Task
OnInitializedAsync()
    {
        data = await
Http.GetStringAsync("api/data");
    }
}
```

- **Registering Services (in `Program.cs`):**

```
builder.Services.AddSingleton<MyService>(
);

// Or

builder.Services.AddScoped<HttpClient>(sp
=>
    new HttpClient { BaseAddress = new
Uri("https://api.example.com/") });
```

8. JavaScript Interop

- **Invoking JavaScript from C#:**

```
@inject IJSRuntime JS

@code {
    private async Task CallJsMethod()
    {
        await JS.InvokeVoidAsync("alert",
"Hello from Blazor!");
    }
}

<button @onclick="CallJsMethod">Call JS
Alert</button>
```

- **Invoking C# from JavaScript:**

```
[JSInvokable]
public static void SayHello(string name)
{
    Console.WriteLine($"Hello, {name}!");
}

// JavaScript:
DotNet.invokeMethodAsync('MyAssembly',
'SayHello', 'Blazor User');
```

9. Forms and Validation

- **Simple Form:**

```
<EditForm Model="@user"
OnValidSubmit="HandleSubmit">
    <DataAnnotationsValidator />
    <ValidationSummary />

    <InputText @bind-Value="user.Name" />
    <ValidationMessage For="@(() =>
user.Name)" />

    <button type="submit">Submit</button>
</EditForm>

@code {
    private User user = new User();

    private void HandleSubmit()
    {
        // Handle form submission
    }
}
```

- **Model with Data Annotations:**

```
public class User
{
    [Required]
    [StringLength(100, MinimumLength =
2)]
    public string Name { get; set; }
}
```

Blazor Project Templates

To help you get started with your Blazor projects, here are several project templates designed for common use cases. These templates serve as a foundation, allowing you to focus on building your application's specific features without having to set up the basic structure from scratch. Each template includes the essential components, layouts, and services needed for its respective use case.

These Blazor project templates are intended to give you a head start on your development projects, allowing you to focus on building the unique features of your application while relying on a solid, pre-built foundation. Whether you're building a dashboard, form builder, or e-commerce site, these templates provide a flexible starting point that you can customize to fit your specific needs.

1. Dashboard Template

Description: A template for creating an interactive, modular dashboard. It includes pre-built components for widgets, charts, and tables, along with a responsive layout.

Features:

- **Modular Widgets:** Reusable widget components with options for drag-and-drop positioning.
- **Charts Integration:** Basic chart components using a library like Chart.js or MudBlazor.
- **Responsive Design:** Layout adjusts to different screen sizes.

- **Data Binding:** Example of binding data to widgets and charts.
- **Real-Time Updates:** Optional integration with SignalR for live data updates.

Project Structure:

```plaintext
BlazorDashboardTemplate/
│
├── Pages/
│   ├── Dashboard.razor          # Main dashboard page
│   ├── WidgetContainer.razor    # Container for dashboard widgets
│   └── RealTimeData.razor       # Example of a widget with real-time data
│
├── Components/
│   ├── Widget.razor             # Reusable widget component
│   ├── ChartWidget.razor        # Widget displaying charts
│   └── TableWidget.razor        # Widget displaying tables
│
├── Services/
│   └── DataService.cs           # Service for fetching data
│
└── wwwroot/
    └── css/
        └── dashboard.css        # Custom CSS for dashboard styling
```

Usage:

```razor
<WidgetContainer>
    <Widget Title="Sales Overview">
        <ChartWidget Data="@SalesData" />
    </Widget>
```

```
    <Widget Title="Active Users">
        <TableWidget Data="@UserData" />
    </Widget>
</WidgetContainer>

@code {
    private List<SalesData> SalesData = ...;
    private List<UserData> UserData = ...;
}
```

2. Form Builder Template

Description: A dynamic form builder template that generates forms based on metadata. Ideal for applications that require flexible data entry forms that can be customized at runtime.

Features:

- **Metadata-Driven Forms:** Generate forms dynamically from JSON or C# classes.
- **Validation:** Built-in support for data annotations and custom validation logic.
- **Field Types:** Support for various input types like text, dropdowns, checkboxes, and date pickers.
- **Responsive Layout:** Form adjusts to different screen sizes.
- **State Management:** Manage form state and validation seamlessly.

Project Structure:

```
plaintext
BlazorFormBuilderTemplate/
│
├── Pages/
│   └── FormBuilder.razor         # Main form
builder page
```

```
├── Components/
│     ├── DynamicForm.razor        # Component to
render dynamic forms
│     ├── InputField.razor         # Reusable
input field component
│     └── ValidationSummary.razor  # Component for
displaying validation messages
│
├── Models/
│     ├── FormField.cs             # Model
representing a form field
│     └── FormMetadata.cs          # Metadata
class for dynamic forms
│
├── Services/
│     └── FormService.cs           # Service for
handling form data and validation
│
└── wwwroot/
      └── css/
            └── formbuilder.css     # Custom CSS
for form styling
```

Usage:

```razor
<DynamicForm Metadata="@FormMetadata"
OnSubmit="HandleSubmit" />

@code {
    private FormMetadata FormMetadata = ...;

    private void HandleSubmit(FormData data) {
        // Handle form submission
    }
}
```

3. E-Commerce Site Template

Description: A template for building a simple e-commerce site. It includes product listing, shopping cart, and checkout pages, along with product and user management features.

Features:

- **Product Catalog:** Display products with pagination, filtering, and sorting.
- **Shopping Cart:** Add to cart functionality with quantity adjustments.
- **Checkout Process:** Multi-step checkout process with payment integration.
- **User Authentication:** Basic user registration and login functionality.
- **Admin Panel:** Manage products and orders.

Project Structure:

```plaintext
BlazorEcommerceTemplate/
│
├── Pages/
│   ├── Index.razor              # Home page
with featured products
│   ├── ProductDetails.razor     # Product
details page
│   ├── Cart.razor               # Shopping
cart page
│   ├── Checkout.razor           # Checkout
page
│   └── Admin/
│       ├── Products.razor       # Admin panel
for managing products
│       └── Orders.razor         # Admin panel
for managing orders
│
├── Components/
│   ├── ProductCard.razor        # Reusable
product card component
```

```
|       ├── CartSummary.razor        # Summary of
items in the cart
|       └── CheckoutForm.razor       # Checkout
form component
|
├── Models/
|       ├── Product.cs               # Product
model
|       ├── Order.cs                 # Order model
|       └── User.cs                  # User model
for authentication
|
├── Services/
|       ├── ProductService.cs        # Service for
handling product data
|       ├── OrderService.cs          # Service for
managing orders
|       └── AuthService.cs           # Service for
user authentication
|
└── wwwroot/
    ├── css/
    |   └── ecommerce.css            # Custom CSS
for styling
    └── images/
        └── product-placeholder.png
```

Usage:

```razor
razor
<ProductCard Product="product"
OnAddToCart="AddToCart" />

@code {
    private List<Product> products = ...;

    private void AddToCart(Product product) {
        // Add product to shopping cart
    }
}
```

How to Use These Templates

1. **Download or Clone the Template:**
   - You can either download the ZIP file or clone the repository if it's available on GitHub.
   - For example:

   ```
   git clone
   https://github.com/yourusername/Bla
   zorDashboardTemplate.git
   ```

2. **Open in Visual Studio:**
   - Open the project in Visual Studio or your preferred IDE.
3. **Customize the Template:**
   - Modify the template according to your specific needs. Update the models, services, and components to match your application's requirements.
4. **Run the Application:**
   - Start the application using `dotnet run` or by pressing `F5` in Visual Studio to see the template in action.
5. **Extend Functionality:**
   - Add new pages, components, or services as your application grows. These templates are designed to be scalable and adaptable.

Resources for Further Learning

As you continue to develop your skills in Blazor and .NET web development, there are numerous resources available to help you stay updated, deepen your knowledge, and explore advanced topics. Below is a curated list of resources that will support your ongoing learning journey.

Official Documentation and Guides

- **Blazor Documentation:** The official Microsoft documentation is the best starting point for learning Blazor. It provides detailed guides, tutorials, and API references.
  - Blazor Documentation
- **.NET API Browser:** This resource allows you to explore the .NET API, including Blazor-specific classes and methods.
  - API Browser

Books and eBooks

- **Blazor in Action** by Chris Sainty: A comprehensive guide to Blazor, covering everything from the basics to advanced topics like performance optimization and component libraries.
- **Blazor Revealed** by Peter Himschoot: This book provides a solid introduction to Blazor, including practical examples and real-world scenarios.
- **ASP.NET Core in Action** by Andrew Lock: While not exclusively focused on Blazor, this book covers ASP.NET Core, which is foundational to Blazor development.

Online Courses and Tutorials

- **Pluralsight - Blazor Courses:** Pluralsight offers a variety of Blazor courses that range from beginner to advanced levels.
  - Pluralsight Blazor Courses
- **Udemy - Complete Blazor Course**: Udemy has several courses on Blazor, including full-stack development with Blazor and .NET Core.
  - Udemy Blazor Courses
- **Microsoft Learn - Blazor Modules:** Microsoft Learn offers free, interactive learning modules on Blazor and other related technologies.
  - Microsoft Learn

Community and Forums

- **Blazor GitHub Repository:** The official Blazor GitHub repository is a great place to explore the source code, track issues, and contribute to the project.
  - Blazor GitHub
- **Blazor Gitter Community:** Engage with the Blazor community in real-time, ask questions, and share your knowledge.
  - Gitter Blazor Community
- **Stack Overflow - Blazor Tag:** Stack Overflow is an excellent platform to ask questions and find answers related to Blazor.
  - Blazor on Stack Overflow

Blogs and Websites

- **Blazor University:** An independent, in-depth resource for learning Blazor, covering a wide range of topics from basic to advanced.

- Blazor University
- **Chris Sainty's Blog:** Chris Sainty regularly blogs about Blazor, sharing tutorials, tips, and insights.
    - Chris Sainty's Blog
- **Daniel Roth's Blog:** As one of the lead developers on the Blazor team, Daniel Roth's blog offers valuable insights and updates on Blazor development.
    - Daniel Roth's Blog

Open-Source Projects and Examples

- **BlazorHero:** A clean architecture template for Blazor WebAssembly built with .NET Core 5.0. It's a great resource to see how a production-ready Blazor application is structured.
    - BlazorHero
- **Blazing Pizza:** A hands-on workshop that demonstrates how to build a Blazor WebAssembly app with SignalR integration.
    - Blazing Pizza
- **MudBlazor:** An open-source component library built on Blazor, providing a range of UI components and utilities.
    - MudBlazor

Conferences and Meetups

- **.NET Conf:** An annual virtual event hosted by Microsoft, covering the latest in .NET, including Blazor.
    - NET Conf
- **Blazor Day:** A free, community-driven virtual conference focusing entirely on Blazor.
    - Blazor Day

- **Local .NET User Groups:** Joining a local .NET user group is a great way to meet other developers, share knowledge, and stay informed about the latest Blazor developments.

Continuous Learning Tools

- **GitHub Actions:** Explore CI/CD for your Blazor projects using GitHub Actions, which is increasingly important for modern development workflows.
  - GitHub Actions
- **Visual Studio Extensions:** Stay updated with the latest Visual Studio extensions for Blazor to enhance your development experience.
  - Visual Studio Marketplace
- **Browser Developer Tools:** Learning to use browser developer tools effectively is crucial for debugging and optimizing Blazor applications.
  - Chrome DevTools

These resources will equip you with the knowledge and tools to continue growing as a Blazor developer. By actively engaging with these materials and communities, you'll stay ahead in the fast-evolving world of Blazor and .NET development. Happy coding!

Glossary of Terms

This glossary provides definitions for key terms and concepts related to Blazor and web development. Understanding these terms will help you navigate the Blazor ecosystem more effectively and enhance your learning experience.

.NET
A free, cross-platform, open-source developer platform for building many different types of applications, including web, mobile, desktop, games, and IoT. Blazor is built on top of the .NET platform.

.NET Core
A cross-platform version of .NET for building websites, services, and console apps. Blazor is a part of the .NET Core ecosystem.

.NET MAUI (Multi-platform App UI)
A framework for building cross-platform applications using a single codebase, targeting Android, iOS, macOS, and Windows. Blazor can be used with .NET MAUI to create hybrid applications.

API (Application Programming Interface)
A set of definitions and protocols for building and integrating application software. APIs allow applications to communicate with each other, and in Blazor, APIs are often used to interact with backend services.

Blazor
A web framework for building interactive web UIs using

C# and .NET. It allows developers to build client-side applications using C# instead of JavaScript.

Blazor Components
Reusable building blocks in Blazor applications. Each component is a piece of UI, encapsulating markup, logic, and styles, and can be nested, reused, and shared across the application.

Blazor Server
A Blazor hosting model where the Blazor application runs on the server and interacts with the client via SignalR. UI updates and event handling occur over a real-time connection, minimizing the amount of code sent to the client.

Blazor WebAssembly (WASM)
A Blazor hosting model where the Blazor application runs directly in the browser using WebAssembly. This model allows for full client-side interactivity without requiring a server connection after the initial load.

CI/CD (Continuous Integration/Continuous Deployment)
A set of practices that automate the processes of building, testing, and deploying applications. CI/CD is crucial for maintaining high-quality software and enabling rapid release cycles in Blazor applications.

CORS (Cross-Origin Resource Sharing)
A security feature implemented in web browsers that restricts how resources on a web page can be requested from another domain outside the domain from which the resource originated. Blazor applications must properly handle CORS when making API calls to external services.

CSHTML

A file extension for Razor pages that combines C# and HTML markup. In Blazor, .razor files replace .cshtml files, but the concept of embedding C# in HTML remains central to Blazor development.

CSS (Cascading Style Sheets)

A stylesheet language used to describe the presentation of a document written in HTML or XML. Blazor supports the use of CSS for styling components and pages.

Data Binding

A mechanism that allows the automatic synchronization of UI elements with the underlying data model. Blazor supports one-way and two-way data binding to simplify the management of UI state.

Dependency Injection (DI)

A design pattern used to achieve Inversion of Control (IoC) between classes and their dependencies. Blazor supports DI out of the box, allowing you to inject services like HTTP clients, state containers, and more into your components.

EventCallback

A type used in Blazor to allow parent components to handle events in child components. It ensures that event handling logic can be passed between components while maintaining proper component encapsulation.

Fluxor

A popular state management library for Blazor based on the Flux architecture. Fluxor provides predictable state management for Blazor applications, making it easier to manage complex UI states.

gRPC

A high-performance, open-source RPC (Remote Procedure Call) framework that can be used for communication between Blazor clients and backend services. It offers advantages over traditional REST APIs, including faster data transfer and built-in support for bi-directional streaming.

HTML (HyperText Markup Language)

The standard markup language for creating web pages and web applications. Blazor components are built using a combination of HTML and C#.

JavaScript Interop

A feature in Blazor that allows C# code to call JavaScript functions and vice versa. This is useful for integrating existing JavaScript libraries and browser APIs into Blazor applications.

JSX

A syntax extension for JavaScript used in React to describe what the UI should look like. Blazor's Razor syntax serves a similar purpose by allowing C# to be embedded in HTML.

Lazy Loading

A design pattern that delays the loading of resources or components until they are actually needed. Blazor supports lazy loading for components and assemblies to improve application performance.

LINQ (Language Integrated Query)

A powerful querying syntax in C# that allows developers to query collections of objects. LINQ is commonly used in Blazor for data manipulation and binding.

MVC (Model-View-Controller)
A design pattern for developing web applications. While Blazor doesn't strictly follow MVC, it shares some concepts, such as separating concerns and promoting a clean structure between data, UI, and logic.

NuGet
A package manager for .NET that enables developers to share and consume code libraries. Blazor components and libraries are often distributed via NuGet.

Razor
A markup syntax for embedding C# code into HTML. Razor is the foundation of Blazor components, enabling dynamic web page generation with a clean, familiar syntax.

REST (Representational State Transfer)
An architectural style for designing networked applications. Blazor applications commonly use REST APIs for data access and communication with backend services.

SignalR
A library for adding real-time web functionality to applications. Blazor Server uses SignalR to manage the communication between the client and server, enabling real-time updates without requiring a full page refresh.

SPA (Single Page Application)
A web application that loads a single HTML page and dynamically updates content as the user interacts with the app. Blazor applications, especially Blazor WebAssembly apps, are typically built as SPAs.

State Management
The process of managing the state of an application, particularly how data flows between the UI and the

business logic. Blazor supports various state management techniques, including cascading values, state containers, and external libraries like Fluxor.

Tag Helpers
A feature in ASP.NET Core that enables server-side rendering of HTML elements with custom logic. While Blazor uses Razor components instead of Tag Helpers, the concept of enhancing HTML elements with server-side logic is similar.

WebAssembly (WASM)
A binary instruction format for a stack-based virtual machine. WebAssembly enables web applications to run at near-native speed by allowing C# code to execute directly in the browser. Blazor WebAssembly uses WASM to run .NET code on the client side.

WebSocket
A communication protocol that provides full-duplex communication channels over a single TCP connection. WebSockets are often used in Blazor Server apps to maintain a persistent connection between the client and server.

XML (eXtensible Markup Language)
A markup language that defines a set of rules for encoding documents in a format that is both human-readable and machine-readable. XML is often used in web services and data interchange, although it's less common in modern Blazor applications which tend to use JSON.

Made in the USA
Columbia, SC
21 November 2024

47209492R00137